Happy Birthday,
Diana —

THE SPIRIT OF REVIVAL

THE
SPIRIT
OF
REVIVAL

DISCOVERING THE WISDOM
OF JONATHAN EDWARDS

ARCHIE PARRISH

AND

R. C. SPROUL

With the Complete, Modernized Text of
The Distinguishing Marks of a Work of the Spirit of God

CROSSWAY BOOKS • WHEATON, ILLINOIS
A DIVISION OF GOOD NEWS PUBLISHERS

The Spirit of Revival

Copyright © 2000 by Archie Parrish

Published by Crossway Books
A division of Good News Publishers
1300 Crescent Street
Wheaton, Illinois 60187

Originally published in 1741 under the title *The Distinguishing Marks of a Work of The Spirit of God Applied to That Uncommon Operation That Has Lately Appeared on the Minds of Many of the People of New England: With a Particular Consideration of the Extraordinary Circumstances with Which This Work is Attended.*

Scripture taken from the HOLY BIBLE: NEW INTERNATIONAL VERSION ®. Copyright © 1973, 1978, 1984 by International Bible Society. Used by permission of Zondervan Publishing House. All rights reserved.

The "NIV" and "New International Version" trademarks are registered in the United States Patent and Trademark Office by International Bible Society. Use of either trademark requires the permission of International Bible Society.

Scripture quotations marked NKJV are from *The New King James Version*, copyright © 1984 by Thomas Nelson, Inc. All rights reserved. Used by permission.

Cover design: Cindy Kiple

First printing, 2000

Printed in the United States of America

ISBN 1-58134-137-7

Library of Congress Cataloging-in-Publication Data

Parrish, Archie 1932-
    The spirit of revival : discovering the wisdom of Jonathan Edwards : with the complete, modernized text of The distinguishing marks of a work of the Holy Spirit / Archie Parrish and R. C. Sproul.
        p.   cm.
Includes bibliographical references.
ISBN 1-58134-137-7 (alk. paper)
    1. Edwards, Jonathan, 1703-1758. Distinguishing marks of a work of the Spirit of God. 2. Great Awakening. 3. Holy Spirit. 4. Revivals.
I. Parrish, Archie, 1932- II. Edwards, Jonathan, 1703-1758. Distinguishing marks of a work of the Spirit of God. III. Title.
BR520.E353 S67 2000
277.3'081—dc21   99-053555
                                                                              CIP

| 15 | 14 | 13 | 12 | 11 | 10 | 09 | 08 | 07 | 06 | 05 | 04 | 03 | 02 | 01 | 00 |
| 15 | 14 | 13 | 12 | 11 | 10 | 9 | 8 | 7 | 6 | 5 | 4 | 3 | 2 | | |

CONTENTS

THE DISTINGUISHING MARKS OF A WORK OF THE SPIRIT OF GOD
by Jonathan Edwards

SECTION I

INDIFFERENT SIGNS:
*Elements That Are Neither Sure Signs of the Spirit
Nor Marks of the Flesh or the Devil*

SECTION II

BIBLICAL SIGNS:
*Distinguishing Scriptural Evidences of a
Work of the Spirit of God*

ACKNOWLEDGMENTS

Many people have helped complete this work. Rev. Mike Ross pointed me to Richard Owen Roberts, and Richard Owen Roberts pointed me to this work of Jonathan Edwards.

Seventeen men in the Marketplace Ministry were the first to urge publication and wider use. I'm especially grateful for the encouragement of Rev. Al LaCour, Wade Williams, Doug Johns, and Rick Ross.

Patsy Rhodes spent countless hours proofreading the early manuscript.

More than 500 pastors over the past four years recruited four to twelve men in Key Covenant Teams and field tested both the text and the small group strategy. Rev. Cal Frett provided materials to more than thirty pastors.

Finally, I want to thank my dear friend R. C. Sproul for his Introduction and overview. And without the commitment and competence of Gary and Diane Hitzfeld, the final manuscript would never have made it to the publisher on time. To all of these, I give a heartfelt thanks.

Archie Parrish

FOREWORD
by Archie Parrish

Revival and Reformation: Today's Greatest Need

When you read R. C. Sproul's Introduction you will see that he makes it abundantly clear that the greatest need in today's world is the revival and reformation of the Christian Church!

I became convinced of this a few years ago and began looking for help on the subject. The last time God moved in global revival was between 1904 and 1910. Since I knew no one who was an eyewitness to that movement, I searched for books dealing with the subject.

I found the literature on revival to be voluminous! Richard Owen Roberts has published an annotated bibliography on revival containing 5,983 titles. In the preface to that volume Roberts comments, "When it comes to literature on the biblical principles of revival . . . there is a paucity of good material."[1] But of Edwards's *Distinguishing Marks of a Work of the Spirit of God,* he says, "This is one of the most important volumes on revival ever published and should be carefully read by every person deeply interested in revival."[2]

Theologian R. C. Sproul, my longtime friend, for years had been telling me how important the writings of Jonathan Edwards were. Roberts's comment moved me to seriously study *The Distinguishing Marks.* As I read, I was challenged by its truth. I was also concerned about the difficulty of deciphering the text.

Edwards lived about 250 years ago. Some of the words he used do not have the same meaning today. His sentences are compound and complex, sometimes extending almost a full page. I had to think long and hard on each page to understand what Edwards was saying. But when I finished the work, I found myself in agreement with Roberts. *Distinguishing Marks* is "must" reading for anyone interested in revival.

This includes laypeople with little or no formal training in theology and people who do not have the time to wade through Edwards's complex sentences and archaic terms. A study of both Scripture and history shows that God usually brings revival through "nobodies from nowhere," humble people who lived in little-known places who in their own time were not considered celebrities. The apostle Paul reminded the Corinthian believers, "Simply consider your own calling, brothers; not many of you were wise, humanly speaking, not many mighty, not many noble. But God has chosen the world's foolish things to put to shame the learned; and God has chosen the weak in the world to shame the strong. God has chosen the world's insignificant and despised people and nobodies in order to bring to nothing those who amount to something, so that nobody may boast in the presence of the Lord" (1 Cor. 1:26-29, *Berkeley*).

Many of the anointed leaders of revival have been young men under thirty years of age. Though Edwards was in his thirties, George Whitefield, a coworker with Edwards, was twenty-two, and Evan Roberts, the primary leader of the Welsh revival, was twenty-four.

For my own benefit, I decided to simplify *Distinguishing*

Marks. I replaced many of the archaic words. I shortened most of the sentences. I changed all of the Scripture references to the *New International Version*. Edwards did not give references for many Scripture allusions; so I added these and also placed many of the texts in the footnotes so they were easily consulted. Then I pulled together an outline for the whole book and made it the bulk of the Table of Contents. While I was doing all this, I was also meeting each week for Bible study with a group of seventeen men. When they discovered what I had done, they asked if the whole group could work through *Distinguishing Marks*. I prepared a guide to facilitate study and discussion in small groups. Then I gave the new work a title to express my prayer and expectation: *Do It Again, Lord—Personal and Church Preparation for the Coming Great Awakening*. That work was the forerunner of this book, *The Spirit of Revival*.

R. C. Sproul for many years has been my theological mentor. Knowing his love for Edwards, I asked him to look over what I had done to this writing of Edwards. He encouraged me to share this with as many people as possible. Word spread to others about the discussion group, and requests began coming in from across the country. So I prepared a Leader's Guide. This Leader's Guide provided the detailed process for establishing and maintaining Key Covenant Teams in the local church. At this printing more than 500 pastors have recruited four to twelve men and spent five weeks reading and discussing this material. The Discussion Guide is printed in the back of this book, and the Leader's Guide is available from Serve International, 4646 North Shallowford Road, Suite 200, Atlanta, Georgia 30338, telephone: 770-642-2449, fax: 770-642-4195.

Edwards wrote *Distinguishing Marks* out of extensive first-hand experience. The Awakening began in 1732. In 1737 he wrote *The Faithful Narrative of the Surpassing Work of God in the Conversion of Many Hundred Souls in Northampton.* The Awakening reached its peak in 1740, and traces of it continued until 1770. Edwards wrote *Distinguishing Marks* in 1741. Thus, he had time to ponder and analyze what was happening.

For this publication, R. C. Sproul has provided a "Historical Introduction," an overview of Edwards's *Distinguishing Marks*.

The purpose of this edited work is to provide truth that will enable today's Christians to understand how to distinguish the work of the Holy Spirit as explained by the apostle John in 1 John 4. By understanding and acting on this truth, believers will grow in personal holiness and will be prepared for the coming revival.

As you study *The Spirit of Revival*, pray that God will once again pour out His Spirit in mighty power, revive His people, and reform His church. May God once again use the truth contained in Edwards's original work to enable His people to discern the work of the Holy Spirit in their individual lives and in His Church. May He give us another Great Awakening—soon!

Archie Parrish
Atlanta, 1999

Footnotes to This Section

1. Richard Owen Roberts, *Revival Literature, an Annotated Bibliography with Biographical and Historical Notices* (Wheaton, Ill.: Roberts Publishers, 1987), p. x.
2. Richard Owen Roberts, *Revival* (Wheaton, Ill.: Roberts Publishers, 1982), p. 150.

INTRODUCTION
by R. C. Sproul

Revival and Reformation

Post tenebras lux . . . "After darkness, light." So read the motto of the Protestant Reformation of the sixteenth century. The titanic theological struggle of that era was a fight to bring the Gospel into the full light of day after years of being consigned to obscurity to the point of eclipse beneath the umbra of the sacerdotal supplanting of it by Rome.

With the rescue of the Gospel from darkness and distortion, a revival was evoked that transcended any revival of faith witnessed either by previous or subsequent periods of Christian history. The Reformation was not merely a Great Awakening; it was the Greatest Awakening to the true Gospel since the Apostolic Age. It was an awakening that demonstrated the power of God unto salvation.

It is noteworthy that this period in history is commonly referred to as the Reformation and not the Revival. What is the difference between *revival* and *reformation*? As the etymologies of the words suggest, *revival* describes a renewal of spiritual life, while *reformation* describes a renewal of the forms and structures of society and culture. It is not possible to have true reformation without first having true revival. The renewal of spiritual life under the power of the Holy Spirit is a *necessary* condition for reformation but not a *sufficient* condition for it. Therefore, though it is not possible to have reformation without revival, it is possible to have revival without reformation. Why is that the case? There are at least two reasons. The first is that revival brings with it the conversion of souls to Christ, who are at the moment of conversion spiritual babes. Infants have little impact on the shaping of cultural institutions. It is when vast numbers of converted people approach maturity in their faith and sanctification that the structures of the world are seriously challenged and changed. If vast numbers of people are converted but remain infantile in their spiritual growth, little impact is made by them on society as a whole. Their faith tends to remain privatized and contained within the confines of the arena of mere religion.

The second reason concerns the scope and intensity of the revival. If the revival is limited in scope and intensity, its impact tends to be restricted to a small geographical area and also tends to be short-lived. Yet it may have rivulets of abiding influence into future generations. Such a rivulet is the work of Jonathan Edwards presented and discussed in this book. The Great Awakening that occurred in New England in the mid-eighteenth century has left an indelible mark on America, though that mark has faded dramatically over time. No one would today confuse New England with a mecca of vibrant gospel faith. Nor is there any danger of the works of Jonathan Edwards pushing any contemporary authors off the *New York Times*'s list of best sellers.

Nevertheless, the influence of Edwards as well as that of the magisterial reformers Luther and Calvin continue to this day. Their words are still in print, and there is a cadre of Christians who devour their writings. The things of which those men of God wrote maintain a vital relevance down to our own day.

William Cooper's original preface to Edwards's *The Distinguishing Marks* describes the state of the church prior to the Great Awakening. It could just as well serve as a commentary for our own times.

The Cultural Context

We live on the far side of a watershed in American history. Our nation has gone through two mighty revolutions since Edwards wrote his treatise. The first revolution was that which yielded the foundation of the United States into an independent republic. Edwards labored before the Revolutionary War that won the independence of the American colonies from the British crown.

In the eighteenth century the western world witnessed two major revolutions—the American Revolution and the French Revolution. The two have often been compared and contrasted by historians. The chief difference between the two may be seen in the root causes of the conflicts.

In the case of the French Revolution, the objective of the revolutionaries was to bring a radical change to French culture including the political institutions, customs, mores, and ethos of the old order. In a sense it was a revolt against the status quo and deeply entrenched traditions. The conflict was one of profound bloodshed accompanied by a reign of terror.

By way of contrast, the American Revolution was not fought to overthrow or destroy the old order but to preserve it. The colonists resisted changes enacted by Parliament that threatened the established American way of life.

Sometimes we tend to forget that America did not begin as

a nation at the end of the eighteenth century. The settlers began the task of colonization of America in the early years of the seventeenth century with the Jamestown settlement in 1607 and the Massachusetts settlement in 1620. We tend to forget that between 1607 and the inauguration of George Washington, more than 175 years of time elapsed, only slightly less time than has transpired between George Washington and William Jefferson Clinton. We tend to telescope our history to the extent that we see Miles Standish and Thomas Jefferson as virtual contemporaries.

The point is, the time that elapsed between the beginning of colonial America and the Revolutionary War was ample time to establish an American way of life with its own traditions, customs, mores, and cultural ethos. Those elements were not suddenly and dramatically overthrown by the American Revolution. Indeed, as is the case with all cultural customs, they were exposed to gradual changes and adaptations—but without radical overthrow until the Second American Revolution.

When I speak of the Second American Revolution I am thinking of the cultural revolution that took place in the decade of the sixties and early seventies. This revolution was far more drastic in its consequences for American life than was the first Revolution. It ushered in a new order that has left our culture gripped in an ongoing cultural war that has a nation divided and fragmented over issues of sexual morality, the relation between church and state, the collapse of the family unit, the emergence of a drug culture, and a radical change in the customs of polite speech. A culture that once embraced normative ethics has given way to an ethos of relativism. The impact on education, law, the press, and virtually every societal institution has been enormous. Clearly we are living in a new order, which some, including myself, view as a new disorder.

It is this cultural context we must keep in view when we speak of spiritual revival and/or reformation. It is this present order, including the state of the church, that we must understand when we seek to find relevance or application for Edwards's work to our own time.

During the same time that the cultural revolution was in high gear, significant events were unfolding within the church. During the decade of the sixties we saw the explosion of the charismatic movement that spread far beyond the confines of Pentecostal churches and penetrated mainline denominations. Subsequently it has become a major force within contemporary evangelicalism. In the years since the sixties we've also seen a large decline in the membership of liberal churches and a corresponding rise in membership in conservative and evangelical churches. Polls indicate a marked increase in the adherents of evangelicalism since 1960.

During the same period we have witnessed a rising involvement of people in occult practices and the advent of New Age philosophy and religion. A new fascination with supernaturalism has slowed the tide of the creeping naturalism so entrenched in the secular culture.

The Relevance of Edwards's Distinguishing Marks

What do these trends signify? Are we in the midst of a major revival? Or are we seeing spurious marks of revival? Here is where the revisiting of Edwards's *Distinguishing Marks* can be most helpful. For us to discern the presence of an authentic revival, we need to know what such a revival would look like.

When signs of revival appear on the landscape of history, one of the first questions that is raised is that of authenticity. Is the revival genuine, or is it a mere outburst of superficial emotion? Do we find empty enthusiasm backed by nothing of substance, or does the enthusiasm itself signal a major work of God? In every recorded revival in church history, the signs that follow it are mixed. The gold is always mixed with dross. Every revival has its counterfeits; distortions tend to raise questions about the real. This problem certainly attended the eighteenth-century Great Awakening in New England, in which Jonathan Edwards was a key figure. His *Distinguishing Marks* provides a careful analysis of that revival, noting its substance as well as its excesses. But the Puritan divine's study of the matter has more relevance than its application to that singular awakening. It provides a map to follow for all such periods of revival and for that reason is of abiding value for us today.

A Preview of Edwards's Distinguishing Marks

Edwards bases his assessment of revival, in the first instance, on an application of the exhortation of 1 John 4:1: "Dear friends, do not believe every spirit, but test the spirits to see whether they are from God, because many false prophets have gone out into the world."

This text functioned as the normative benchmark for Edwards. Ironically, the biblical mandate here is a call to *unbe-*

lief. Certainly this call to unbelief does not summon us to the faithlessness of the ungodly; it is not a repudiation of true biblical faith. Rather, it is a red alert against the beguiling force of credulity, a readiness to believe on the basis of insufficient evidence. As Augustine had done centuries before, Edwards noted a difference between faith and credulity. Credulity is faith without substance, an easy-believism that lacks critical judgment and consequently discernment.

Any claim to spiritual power is to be tested to see if the claim is validated by the work of God. This rests on the axiom that not all spirits are holy. The Holy Spirit is also the Spirit of Truth whose operation is validated by the truth of Scripture that He Himself inspired and illuminates.

The testing of the spirits is made necessary by the presence of false prophets, who are both alluring and numerous. The Israelites' greatest threat in Old Testament times was never the warring nations that surrounded them and often invaded their borders from the outside. It was always the threat of the false prophets within their own gates. The false prophets of Israel had their own "revivals." Their congregations tended to be much larger than the true prophets' because their message and their religion had strong popular appeal. They preached a message that tickled the ears of those who had "itchy ears" but did not have ears to hear the Word of God.

The "worship" offered by false prophets was the worship of idolatry in which the creature was exalted above the Creator. Such worship was popular with the people but repugnant to God. We see a glimpse of this in Exodus 32:

And when Joshua heard the noise of the people as they
shouted, he said to Moses, "There is a noise of war in the
camp." But he said: "It is not the noise of the shout of
victory, nor the noise of the cry of defeat, but the sound
of singing I hear." So it was, as soon as he came near the
camp, that he saw the calf and the dancing.

—vv. 17-19, NKJV

The noise that Joshua heard was not the noise of battle. It
was the noise of joyful religious celebration. The event in view was
one of the best-attended religious gatherings recorded in the Old
Testament. It was the noise of jubilant worship coupled with
unbridled religious zeal. But the object of the worship and the
focal point of the zeal was not God but a golden calf. This was not
reformation but deformation; it was not the experience of revival
or new spiritual life but the expression of spiritual death. Moses
reported this to God, saying, "Oh, these people have committed
a great sin, and have made for themselves a god of gold!" (v. 31,
NKJV). The response of God to this event, which was "a great
sin" rather than a great awakening, was that "the LORD plagued
the people because of what they did with the calf which Aaron
made" (v. 35).

Edwards warns that the influence, operations, and gifts of
the Holy Spirit are aped and mimicked by Satan. That is why it
is necessary to provide marks that can help us distinguish between
the true Spirit of God and false spirits. Without such distinguishing marks the church is vulnerable to delusions and their dire
consequences.

Negative Marks

Edwards begins by following the *via negationis* or "the way of negation." That is, before he proceeds to affirm positively what are the true marks of revival, he first spends time in Section I observing what are *not* (or at least not necessarily) signs of the work of the Spirit of God. Then he quickly moves in Section II to the *positive signs* that are evidences of a true work of the Spirit of God. His presentation of the positive signs flows from his exposition of the text of 1 John 4.

Edwards gives attention to one of the most controversial aspects that attended the awakening in New England, the matter of the *bodily effects* wrought by the Spirit of God upon those under His influence. Here Edwards is careful to note that a true work of God cannot be judged by the bodily or emotional reactions of those who receive this work.

The Bible does not provide a uniform formula for the proper physical or emotional reactions to the presence of the Holy Spirit. The presence of tears, convulsions, jerking, laughter, etc. are no measure of the Spirit's presence. When we canvass the Scripture to see how the saints reacted to the outpouring of the Spirit, we see no prescribed form of bodily behavior. Habakkuk had a quivering lip and a trembling belly. Others fell to the ground as though dead. Some wept, some sang, some were reduced to stunned silence. In light of the diversity of human personalities and indeed the very nature of man, the presence or absence of these responses is no true test of the authenticity of the Spirit's work. However, I hasten to add that though a wide variety of emotional responses may be detected in Scripture by those who encounter the living

God, there is at least one emotion that may safely be excluded
from the list—namely, boredom. It is hardly possible for a creature
made in the image of God to be awakened or revived by the Spirit
of God and be bored in the process.

The presence of *"much noise about the Christian faith"* is
viewed by Edwards as no argument against true revival. When the
Spirit of God moves, not only are waters stirred up, but people are
as well. Such stirring is a common indication of the controversy
that attends the bold proclamation of the Gospel. Just as the apostolic preaching of the first century stirred up mighty opposition
against it, so in any generation the resistance to the Gospel will
be made manifest. The kingdom of Christ is in direct conflict
with the kingdom of Satan and the kingdoms of this world. The
Christian faith is a disturbance of the peace. But the peace it disturbs is a carnal peace, a peace that is wrongfully "at ease in Zion"
(Amos 6:1, NKJV). Though Christ is the Prince of Peace and gives
His peace as a legacy to His people ("My peace I give you," John
14:27), it must not be forgotten that Christ did not come to bring
a carnal peace; rather, His coming provokes a crisis in the midst of
the world.

The more at peace the Church is with the world, the more
worldly the Church becomes. It may be said that in one sense the
worst thing that ever happened to the Church was the Edict of
Constantine in the fourth century, by which Christianity was
declared the official religion of the Roman Empire. For the first
time in history the Church had something to lose. It was now
acceptable, and its new status inclined it to compromise in order
to preserve public acceptability. This is the curse of mainline

churches that quench the Spirit in order to protect their own social acceptability.

The *stirring up of imaginations and emotions* is also no argument against authentic awakening. We need look no further than to human nature to account for zealous excesses of behavior, especially among infant Christians. Under the powerful influence of the Spirit people can easily become carried away with zeal and emotion. Edwards says:

> They may have soul-ravishing views of the beauty and love of Christ. And they might have their normal strength overpowered. Therefore, it is not at all strange that with so many affected in this manner, there should be some people of a particular makeup who would have their imaginations thus affected.

We think of Jeremiah, who under the influence of the Spirit of God cried out, "O LORD, you deceived me, and I was deceived. You overpowered me and prevailed."[1] Here the prophet exhibits an extraordinary grasp of the obvious. Never was an inspired redundancy so evident. If one is deceived by God, it is plain that he is deceived. When the Almighty overwhelms a person, it takes no acute deduction of logic to realize that they are indeed overwhelmed.

Arguments proved often from *example* rather than from careful reasonings during a strong visitation of the Spirit of God are likewise no arguments against such visitations. Great impressions of religious affection are often expressed in actions rather than words. Edwards remarks: "In some cases, the language of action is much more clear and convincing than words."

This is consistent with the injunction of James that we must show our faith by our works. The impact of example or modeling was clear in the Apostolic Age as well as during the Reformation. The Scripture calls attention to the example set by the Old Testament saints in Hebrews 11.

Edwards then notes that those exposed to the operation of the Spirit may be *guilty of rash acts and unconventional conduct*. The Spirit tends to overthrow human conventions. Edwards declares, "The end for which God pours out His Spirit is to make men holy, and not to make them politicians." This is consistent with the biblical call to not conform to this world but to be transformed by the renewing of the mind.

Even rash acts that are contrary to the Word of God do not disprove the presence of revival. In the New Testament, the Corinthian congregation, where abuses attended the awaking of the people of God, is a case in point. The Spirit who works sanctification in the believer does not do it all at once. There is dross with the gold, tares with the wheat.

The new convert may easily be *puffed up and exhibit an overconfidence with his or her boldness*. Though such zeal may be mixed with corruption, at least it is not the lukewarmness that Edwards calls vile. The zeal of the new convert can lead to an immature spirit of censure and/or to legalistic practices, which though contrary to the Word of God are common in the midst of a true work of God.

The true work of God may be *intermixed with errors in judgment and delusions of Satan*. The true miracles of God are often countered by the false or counterfeit miracles of Satan, such as were seen in the days of Moses when he encountered the magicians of Pharaoh's court. As Edwards indicates, "The kingdom of God and the kingdom of the devil remain for a while together in the same heart."

The errors or practices that attend true revival may be *gross and scandalous*, but such things may be expected in any time of reformation. Heresies abounded in the early church. The practice of Nicholas the deacon produced the heretical sect bearing his name, the Nicolaitans. From the Gnostics of the early church to the extremists of the Reformation, the pattern is similar. Edwards said of the extremists of the sixteenth century, "It was as if the reformation had been the sun to give heat and warmth to those worms and serpents to crawl out of the ground."

That *ministers may terrorize people by insisting on the reality of hell and the dreadful judgment of the holy law of God* is also no argument against the work of the Spirit. Edwards is known for his own "scare theology" and has been branded as a sadist for his fire-and-brimstone preaching. But a true sadist, if he believed in hell, would take delight in persuading people there is no hell. That Edwards truly believed in the biblical doctrine of hell is without question. He was concerned that because people lacked a sense of dread of hell, they did not take due care to avoid it. It is as reasonable for preachers to warn against hell as it would be for a sentinel to warn of an approaching army or a weatherman an approaching tornado. Indeed, for a minister to warn of impending disaster in a cold manner, with no emotion or sense of urgency, would be a contradiction. Edwards strongly advocated the preaching of the Gospel but insisted that it was also necessary to preach the law. Without a knowledge of the law, the good news of the Gospel is perceived as no real news. The bad news of the law is what reveals the good news of the Gospel. Edwards says, "Some say it is unreasonable to frighten people into heaven. But I think it is reasonable to try to frighten people away from hell."

Positive Marks

Next Edwards turns to the positive marks or biblical signs of true revival. The first positive mark is seen in *the elevated level of people's esteem for Jesus*. Edwards follows the Reformation's emphasis on the work of the Holy Spirit in the application of the work of Christ in our redemption. It is the chief ministry of God the Holy Spirit to bring people to God the Son and apply His work to them. In a true outpouring of the Holy Spirit people are never led to a unitarianism of the Third Person of the Trinity. A preoccupation with the Holy Spirit without a view of Christ is not the desire of the Holy Spirit Himself. Edwards remarks:

> The person to whom the Spirit gives testimony and for whom He raises their esteem must be Jesus—the one who appeared in the flesh. No other Christ can stand in his place. No mystical, fantasy Christ! No light within—as the spirit of Quakers extols—can diminish esteem of and dependence upon an outward Christ. The Spirit who gives testimony for this historical Jesus and leads to Him can be no other than the Spirit of God.

In his epistle John is keenly concerned to distinguish between Christ and antichrist. The concept of antichrist is often misunderstood in our day. We tend to perceive the image of antichrist simply in terms of those who vehemently oppose Christ. We use the Greek prefix *anti* almost exclusively to mean "against." But the "anti" of antichrist can also be translated to mean "in place of." To be sure, anyone who is a substitute for Christ is at the same time one who stands *against* Christ.

Here we see something of the subtlety of the spirit of antichrist. It can be disguised as an angel of light, garbed in the clothing of piety. Almost daily we hear the dictum "No creed but Christ" or "I don't need to know any doctrine. All I need to know is Christ." These words can formulate the creed of antichrist. The Holy Spirit is the Author of the Book that informs us of the identity of the real, historical Jesus. Scripture works hard to set forth the real Christ. The creeds are merely attempts to preserve this biblical portrait and to protect it from distortions. When a person says, "All I need to know is Jesus—doctrine isn't important," we should immediately ask in reply, "Who is Jesus?" The moment a person begins to answer that question, the person is inescapably involved with doctrine.

To the Christian, doctrine is unavoidable. Ours is never a choice between doctrine and no doctrine, but between sound doctrine and false doctrine. This is nowhere more urgent than when we are talking about the Christ, who is the object of our faith. It is not only liberal scholarship that has turned away from the historical Jesus by viewing the quest for Him as a fool's errand and giving us in His place an existential Jesus, a Marxist Jesus, or a mere teacher of ethical values. "Evangelical" religion can also replace the biblical Christ with a Savior who is not also Lord or a caricature that bears the image of the vested interests of particular institutions, religious organizations, or religious subcultures.

True revival under the impetus of the Holy Spirit cuts through the fantasies and drives us to the biblical and historical Christ—and never to a substitute. Any substitute Jesus, no matter how dripping in piety, is never Christ but is always antichrist.

The second mark Edwards describes is that the Holy Spirit operates *against the interests of Satan's kingdom.* In simple terms this means that the Spirit works against sin. No revival has ever eliminated sin, but all true revivals check and curb sin. The Spirit convicts us of sin and leads us into sanctification. In this convicting operation the consciences of people are awakened from dogmatic slumber. Satan desires that the consciences of people be seared. When the conscience is awakened, the interests of people turn away from lusts and are inclined afresh to the things of God.

Some polls have indicated that in major ethical areas of concern, there is little if any discernible difference in the behavior patterns of professing Christians in America and those of the secular culture with respect to such matters as divorce, abortion, pre- and extramarital sexual relationships, etc. If these polls are accurate, they would indicate that we are far removed from revival.

The third mark is that the Holy Spirit causes *greater regard for the Holy Scriptures.* Edwards argues that a spirit of delusion will not incline people to seek direction at the mouth of God.

Perhaps there has never been a time in the history of the church when the Bible has been subjected to greater attack and criticism than it has in the past 200 years. The higher criticism that reached such wide proportions in the nineteenth century has left its mark on the contemporary Christian community. Near the turn of this century the Dutch theologian Abraham Kuyper remarked that biblical criticism had degenerated into biblical vandalism.

Virtually every Protestant creed has affirmed confidence in the divine origin and authority of Scripture. This was the direct fruit of the Reformation principle of *sola scriptura*. Yet this uniform conviction of historic Protestantism has been all but abandoned in the so-called mainline churches of American Protestantism. Indeed, many of the splinter groups that have divided from mainline denominations have done so precisely over the issue of biblical authority.

However, though we see strong affirmations of the inspiration and inerrancy of the Bible in evangelical churches, there are many evidences of defection from the historic view of Scripture even there. The controversy chronicled by Harold Lindsell in his book *The Battle for the Bible* is still being waged within evangelicalism.

Perhaps what is even more alarming is that even within churches and organizations that still profess a high view of Scripture, there is an alarming ignorance of the content of Scripture. For many, being "led by the Spirit" means being led by some inner light or impulse rather than by the Spirit's testimony to the written Word of God. Edwards says, "And accordingly we see it common in enthusiasts who oppose Christ that they depreciate this written rule and set up the light within their souls or some other rule above it."

Edwards gives as his fourth mark "*the words used in addressing the opposite spirits.*" Appealing still to 1 John 4, he speaks of the sixth verse: "The Spirit of truth and the spirit of falsehood." We recall that before Pontius Pilate Christ declared: "For this cause I was born, and for this cause I have come into the world, that I should bear witness to the truth. Everyone who is of the truth hears my voice.[2]" In light of these words of Jesus, it is clear that His cause is the cause of truth. One cannot be enrolled in the cause of Christ and despise truth. The devil works for the cause of the lie, and as the father of lies he works on behalf of falsehood and error. No true revival can lead Christians to a cavalier attitude toward the truth of God. Luther insisted that whenever the Gospel was clearly proclaimed, controversy would surely follow. The only way to avoid controversy is to avoid the Gospel.

Francis Schaeffer frequently spoke of the necessity of antithesis in the Christian life. That is, for every truth there is a corresponding falsehood. A Christian is known not only by what he believes or affirms, but also by what he rejects and denies. This posture of antithesis is on a collision course with modern theories of relativism. A revived Christian Church will be marked not only by what it affirms but also by its courage to deny truth's antithesis.

The fifth mark is that the Spirit produces *a spirit of love to God and to man.* In this mark we encounter vintage Jonathan Edwards. His entire ministry was captured by a concern for true religious affections. As cerebral as Edwards was, in the final analysis his relationship to Christ was expressed as an affair of the heart. He never tired of speaking of the "excellency" of Christ as the chief object of the believer's delight. It is the Spirit of God who awakens within our souls a true love for God. Speaking of this work of the Holy Spirit Edwards writes: "He makes the attributes of God as revealed in the Gospel and manifested in Christ delightful objects of contemplation. He makes the soul long after God and Christ—after their presence and communion, acquaintance with them and conformity to them; and to live to please and honor them is the spirit that quells contentions among men. He gives a spirit of peace and goodwill."

Here Edwards sees the fulfillment of the reality announced by angels to the shepherds of Bethlehem. This is not the mutual bonds of affections by which heretics and cultists are drawn to mutual admiration among themselves, like honor among thieves, but rather the love that is born in the souls of wretched sinners who know their own wretchedness and cleave to the grace of God whose fellowship they enjoy.

Applications

After discussing these five positive signs, Edwards turns his attention to the application section of his treatise, following the normal structure of his sermons. In Section III he notes the *practical inferences* he draws from his study.

The first inference is that *the recent extraordinary influences were from the Spirit of God*. These influences are judged both by rules and by facts. He points to the facts that correspond to the rules of Scripture—namely, that the positive signs of true awakening he set forth earlier in his treatise are indeed widely evident. They are public and also not confined to remote areas. He cites his own eyewitness experience of the phenomena. He cites his personal awareness of multitudes who have been awakened. "Some have been in great distress from a foreboding of their sin and misery. Others have been overcome with a sweet sense of the greatness, wonderfulness, and excellency of divine things." He points both to the sober signs of awakening as well as delusions and irregularities that attended them and calls for the *promotion of the recent working of the Spirit of God*. Regarding the aforementioned irregularities and delusions, he says, "If they wait to see a work of God without difficulties and stumbling blocks, it will be like a fool waiting at the riverside to have the water all run by. A work of God without stumbling blocks is never to be expected."

To focus on the difficulties that attend genuine revival is to miss the manifold blessings that are poured out by it. It would have meant, for Edwards, missing the visitation of God to New England.

Finally, Edwards turns his attention not to the critics of the Great Awakening, but to its friends. He calls the friends of the work to *self-diligence*. He provides an exhortation to them to avoid the errors and misconduct that characteristically accompany revival. He warns of those who will oppose them and counsels them to be wise as serpents and harmless as doves. He especially warns against the danger of pride, saying:

> Pride is the worst viper in the heart. It is the first sin that ever entered into the universe. It lies lowest of all in the foundation of the whole building of sin. Of all lusts, it is the most secret, deceitful, and unsearchable in its ways of working. It is ready to mix with everything. Nothing is so hateful to God, contrary to the spirit of the Gospel, or of so dangerous consequence. There is no one sin that does so much to let the devil into the hearts of the saints and expose them to his delusions.

He cites the errors of those who suppose that in their imaginations and impressions they have received direct messages from heaven.

Claims to special divine revelations are not so much a sign of super-spirituality as they are of evangelical or pietistic megalomania. The days of prophets and apostles, genuine agents of revelation, are past. Such claims today are spurious and exceedingly dangerous. To cloak one's desires, hunches, or opinions in such claims is to make use of a godless form of persuasion. What does one say to the person who claims, "The Lord told me to do this"? To use such devices is to place oneself above criticism by bathing one's opinions in divine sanction.

The extraordinary gifts of the Apostolic Age are not required today. It is the ordinary influence of the grace of God that should capture our attention. Edwards says:

> The greatest privilege of the prophets and apostles was not their being inspired and working miracles, but their eminent holiness. . . . The extraordinary gifts are worthless without the ordinary sanctifying influences.

Edwards declared that he neither expected nor desired the restoration of the miraculous gifts in the church. He said:

> For my part, I had rather enjoy the sweet influences of the Spirit. I had rather show Christ's spiritual divine beauty, infinite grace, and dying love. I had rather draw forth the holy exercises of faith, divine love, sweet complacence, and humble joy in God. I had rather experience all this for one quarter of an hour than to have prophetical visions and revelations the whole year.

Edwards gives great caution to those who are preoccupied with the extraordinary. The danger is that such a quest becomes a substitute for diligent learning of the things of God. Such learning requires discipline and labor. To function as teachers, preachers, and Christian leaders we must advance to maturity as Christians. In this enterprise there is no substitute for diligent instruction. The judgment of discernment, both for what comprises sound doctrine and sound behavior, comes from being diligent students of the Word of God. Edwards had little use for the ripping of the Spirit away from the Word. Again, the testimony of the saints and the axiom with which Edwards began his treatise is that of subjecting experience to the Scripture. In the Scripture we meet the wisdom of God, which is able to judge all things. He writes:

> The longer I live, the less I wonder that God keeps it as his right to try the hearts of the children of men. Also I wonder less that God directs that this business should be let alone till harvest. I adore the wisdom of God! In His goodness to me and my fellow creatures, He has not committed this great business into our hands.

This practical warning is directed against those who make harsh and precipitous judgments against other Christians. We do not have the capacity to judge the souls of men. That is the prerogative of God. Though not eschewing the proper procedures for necessary church discipline or the need to speak out against error, Edwards is careful to guard the boundaries established by God. Our discernment is always limited. Even those who oppose a true work of God must be dealt with without raging anger. We are to exercise such rebuke with gentleness and prudence.

The work of the Holy Spirit is always a work among sinners. What is true for others is likewise true for ourselves. Though He leads us to holiness, it is a leading out of corruption. That corruption remains, at least in part, until our glorification at His hands. To demand from others what the Spirit Himself patiently endures is to exalt ourselves above God.

The practice of godliness is a practice that is to be informed by Scripture and tempered by the work of the Holy Spirit within us. If we have been awakened, that awakening should bring with it an acute awareness that in many respects we are still aslumber.

The church in our day can profit mightily from a close scrutiny of the insight provided for us by Edwards's careful evaluation of the distinguishing marks of a true revival. He gives us a road map to follow lest we twist and turn into the detours of destruction.

My hope is that the republishing of this work by the Puritan divine will effect a rekindling of zeal for authentic revival and reformation in our day.

R. C. Sproul
Orlando, 1999

FOOTNOTES TO THIS SECTION

1. Jeremiah 20:7a.
2. John 18:37 (NKJV).

PREFACE
by William Cooper

THE DISTINGUISHING MARKS
OF A WORK OF THE SPIRIT OF GOD
by Jonathan Edwards

State of the Church at the Time of the Reformation

At the time of the Reformation, the gospel light broke in upon the church. It drove away the clouds of anti-Christian darkness that covered the Church. The power of divine grace followed the preaching of the Word so that it had visible success in the conversion and building of souls. The blessed fruits appeared in the hearts and lives of those who professed faith. That was one of "the days of the Son of man." Then the exalted Redeemer rode forth in His glory and majesty on the white horse of the pure Gospel, "conquering and to conquer." The bow in His hand was like that of Jonathan; it returned not empty.

The Recent Dead and Barren State of the Church

Now for a great while, it has been a dead and barren time without fruit in all the churches of the Reformation. The showers of blessing have been restrained. The influence of the Spirit stopped. The Gospel has not had any famous success. Conversions have been rare and dubious. Few sons and daughters have been born to God. The hearts of Christians are not as lively, warm, and refreshed under the ordinances of the Word and sacraments as they have been.

The Christian faith has been in this sad state in this land for many years. There are one or two well-known exceptions. This sad state is acknowledged by all who have any spiritual awareness. Faithful ministers and serious Christians lament this fact. This sad state of the church is a constant petition in our public prayers. From Sabbath to Sabbath we pray, "God, pour out Your Spirit upon us, and revive Your work in the midst of the years." Our government has appointed annual fast days. Besides these, most of the churches have set apart days in which to seek the Lord by prayer and fasting, that He would "come and rain down righteousness upon us."

The Present Extraordinary Pouring Out of the Spirit

And now, "Behold! The Lord whom we have sought has suddenly come to His temple." The period of grace we are now under exceeds all that we or our fathers have ever seen. In some situations it is so wonderful that I doubt there has been the like since the extraordinary pouring out of the Spirit immediately after our Lord's ascension. The apostolic times seem to have returned upon us. There has been a great display of the power and grace of the divine Spirit in the assemblies of His people. The Spirit has given witness to the Word of the Gospel.

Anointed Preachers

A number of preachers have appeared among us to whom God has given a large measure of His Spirit. They are like Barnabas, "a good man, and full of the Holy Ghost and of faith."[1] They preach the Gospel of God's grace everywhere with exceptional zeal and power.

They insist on the doctrines of the Reformation under whose influence the power of godliness so flourished in the last century. Their preaching mainly turns on the important points of humanity's guilt, corruption, and impotence. They equally stress supernatural regeneration by the Spirit of God and free justification by faith in the righteousness of Christ and the new birth.

Their preaching is not with the enticing words of man's wisdom. Rather, they speak wisdom among them that are perfect. Burning love for Christ and souls warms their breasts and energizes their work. God makes His ministers flames of fire in His service. His Word in their mouths has been "as a fire, and as a hammer that breaks the rock in pieces." In most places where they labor, God has clearly worked with them and "confirmed the Word by signs following." This much power and presence of God in Christian gatherings has not been known since God set up His sanctuary among us. He has indeed "glorified the house of His glory."

The Extraordinary Extent of the Work

This work is also truly extraordinary in its extent. It is present in varying degrees in the several provinces that cover hundreds of miles on this continent. "He sends forth His commandment on earth! His Word runs very swiftly." It has spread in some of the populous towns, "the chief places of social gathering and business." And—blessed be God—it has visited the seats of learning, both here and in a neighboring colony. Oh, may the Holy Spirit constantly dwell in our devoted youth. May He form them as polished shafts so that when they shall be called out to service, they shall be able to successfully fight the Lord's battles against the powers of darkness!

Extraordinary Numbers

This work is extraordinary also in the numbers who have been the subjects of its operation. Stupid sinners have been awakened by hundreds. The inquiry, "What must I do to be saved?" has been general in some places. In our city last winter, thousands were under spiritual conviction like they had never felt before.

A Remarkable Variety of People

The work has been remarkable also for the variety of people that have been under its influence. They have been of *all ages*. Some *elderly* persons have been snatched as brands out of the fire and made trophies of divine mercy. They have been born to God, though out of due time, as the apostle speaks in his own case.[2]

But here, with us, the work has focused mostly among the *young*. Lively young people have been made to bow like willows to the Redeemer's scepter. Out of the mouths of babes and little children has God ordained to Himself praise to still the enemy and the avenger.

People of *all ranks and degrees* have been under the Spirit's influence—some of the great and rich; but more of the low and poor.

Some of those touched by the Spirit come from *other countries and nations*.

Various Qualities and Conditions

They are of all qualities and conditions. They are the most *ignorant*, foolish people of the world, babes in knowledge. They have been made wise unto salvation and taught those heavenly truths that have been hid from the wise and prudent. Some of the *learned* and knowing among men have had those things revealed to them by the Father in heaven that flesh and blood do not teach. Some held modern opinions and had only the polite religion of the present times. Their prejudices were conquered. Their sensual reasoning was overcome. Their understandings were made to bow to gospel mysteries. They now receive the truth as it is in Jesus. Their faith no longer "stands in the wisdom of man but in the power of God." Some of the most *rude and disorderly* are becoming regular in their behavior and sober in all things. The *overconfident and shallow* are becoming earnest and serious.

Some of the *greatest sinners* appear now to be real saints. Drunkards have become temperate. Fornicators and adulterers now have pure conduct. Swearers and profane persons have learned to fear that glorious and fearful name, THE LORD THEIR GOD. *Sensual worldlings* have been made to seek first the kingdom of God and His righteousness. Yes, *those who treated this work with contempt* and those who mocked it and its agents have come under its conquering power. Some of these people have gone to hear the preachers as some did Paul. They came to Paul saying, "What will this babbler say?" But they were not able to resist the power and the Spirit with which he spoke. Likewise, today men have trembled under the Word and gone away from it weeping. Afterward they cling to the preacher, as Dionysius the Areopagite did cling to Paul.[3] Various instances of this kind have come to my knowledge.

The *virtuous and civil* have been convinced that morality is not to be relied on for life, and so motivated, to seek the new birth and a vital union with Jesus Christ by faith. *Those who merely profess formal religion* have also been awakened out of their dead formalities when brought under the power of godliness. They have turned from their false confidence and came to build their hope only on the Mediator's righteousness.

At the same time many of the *children of God* have been greatly quickened and refreshed. They have been awakened out of their slumbering state and moved to diligently make their calling and election sure. They have had special, reviving, and sealing times.

This is how extensive and general the divine influence has been at this glorious season.

The Uniformity of the Work

One thing more is worthy of remark. This is the uniformity of the work. I have received letters and have had conversations with ministers and others who live in different parts of the land where this work is going on. By these accounts the work is the same in all places. The method of the Spirit's work on people's minds is the same though the circumstances vary. Conversion is the same work wherever it is accomplished. In this extraordinary season God is pleased to carry on the work of His grace in a more observable and glorious manner. He carries on His work in a way that causes the world to take notice. At such a time as this, it seems reasonable to suppose that there may be some particular appearances in the work of conversion that are not common at other times. Some circumstances attending the work may be carried to an unusual degree and height. If it were not so, the work of the Lord would not be so much regarded and spoken of, and God would not have so much of the glory of it. Nor would the work itself be likely to spread so fast. God has evidently made use of example and discourse in carrying it on.

The Endurance of Those Upon Whom the Spirit Works

So far as we have been able to observe the fruits of this work, they appear to be lasting. I do not mean that none have lost their faith, or that there are no instances of hypocrisy and apostasy. Scripture and experience lead us to expect these at such a time. I am surprised and thankful that, as yet, there have been no more. But I mean that a great number of those who have been awakened are still seeking and striving to enter at the strait gate. Most of those who have been thought to be converted continue to give evidence of being new creatures. They seem to cleave to the Lord with full purpose of heart.

Visible Evidence of the Spirit's Work

Taverns and meetings that have always proved unfriendly to serious godliness are much less frequented. Many have simplified their dress and apparel to make them look more like the followers of the humble Jesus. It has been both surprising and pleasant to see that some younger women have put off the "bravery of their ornaments." They seek the inward glories of the "King's daughter." The Christian faith is now much more the subject of conversation at friends' houses than ever I knew it. The doctrines of grace are espoused and relished. Private religious meetings are greatly multiplied. The public assemblies (especially preaching) are much better attended. Listeners were never so attentive and serious. There is indeed an extraordinary appetite after the "sincere milk of the Word."

It is more than a year since an evening sermon was set up in this town. There are now several—two every Tuesday and Friday evening. Some of our most spacious houses are well filled with hearers. By their looks and deportment, they seem to come to hear, that their souls might live. One evening in God's courts is esteemed better than many elsewhere. There is also frequent seeking of pastors in private. Our hands continue full of work, and many times we have more than we can deal with distinctly and separately.

Thankful for Edwards

Many, I believe, will be thankful for Jonathan Edwards's publication. Those who have already entertained favorable thoughts of this work will be confirmed by it, and the doubting may be convinced and satisfied. But if there are any who cannot, after all, see the signatures of a divine hand on the work, it is to be hoped they will be prevailed on to not censure and to stop their oppositions lest "haply they should be found even to fight against God."

Prayer

I will conclude now with my prayer. May the worthy author of this discourse long be continued a burning and shining light in the golden candlestick where Christ has placed him. May he from there spread his light through these provinces! May the divine Spirit, whose cause is here defended, accompany this and the other valuable publications of His servant with His powerful influences. May they promote the Redeemer's interest, serve the ends of vital faith, and so add to the author's present joy and future crown!

W. Cooper
Boston
November 20, 1741

FOOTNOTES TO THIS SECTION

1. Acts 11:24, KJV.
2. 1 Corinthians 15:8.
3. Acts 17:18, 34.

THE DISTINGUISHING MARKS
OF A WORK OF THE SPIRIT OF GOD

By Jonathan Edwards

Dear friends, do not believe every spirit, but test the spirits to see whether they are from God, because many false prophets have gone out into the world.

—1 John 4:1

In the apostolic age there was the greatest outpouring of the Spirit of God that ever was. This outpouring was in both His extraordinary influences and gifts and His ordinary operations—in convincing, converting, enlightening, and sanctifying the souls of men. But as the influences of the true Spirit abounded, so counterfeits did also abound. The devil was abundant in mimicking both the ordinary and extraordinary influences of the Spirit of God. Countless passages of the apostles' writings make this clear. The devil's mimicking made it necessary for the Church of Christ to have rules, distinguishing and clear marks, by which she might safely distinguish the true from the false without danger of being imposed upon. The purpose of 1 John, chapter 4 is to give these rules. Here we have this matter more specifically and fully treated than anywhere else in the Bible. The apostle is determined to give the Church of God marks of the true Spirit. These marks are plain and safe and well suited to practical use. That the subject might be clearly and sufficiently handled, he insists upon practical use throughout the chapter. It is amazing! What is here said is so little noticed in this extraordinary day. There is such an unusual and wide operation on the minds of people. There is such a variety of opinions concerning these marks, and so much talk about the work of the Spirit.

As the apostle introduces his reasoning, he mentions the indwelling of the Spirit as the sure evidence of an interest in Christ. "Those who obey his commands live in him, and he in them. And this is how we know that he lives in us: We know it by the Spirit he gave us" (1 John 3:24). From this truth we may infer that the design of the apostle is to give marks by which to distinguish the true Spirit from the false. We must distinguish between His extraordinary gifts of prophecy and miracles and His ordinary influences on the minds of His people. Christians' union to Christ, and their being built up in Him, is also seen from the marks that are given, which we shall consider below.

The words of the text introduce the distinguishing signs of the true Spirit and the false spirit. Before the apostle goes on to lay down these signs, he exhorts Christians first against being gullible and being quick to admit every deceptively attractive phenomenon as the work of a true Spirit. "Dear friends, do not believe every spirit, but test the spirits, to see whether they are from God." And second, he shows that there were many counterfeits. "Because many false prophets have gone out into the world." Not only did they pretend to have the Spirit of God in His extraordinary gifts of inspiration, but also they pretended to be the great friends and favorites of heaven, to be noteworthy, holy persons. They also claimed to have much of the ordinary saving, sanctifying influences of the Spirit of God on their hearts.

Hence we are to look upon these words as the direction to examine and try their pretenses regarding the Spirit of God in both these respects.

My design, therefore, at this time is to show what are the true, certain, and distinguishing evidences of a work of the Spirit of God. By these evidences we may safely judge any operation we find in ourselves or see in others. And here I would observe that we are to take the Scriptures as our guide in such cases. This great and standing rule is without error and is sufficient. God has given this rule to His Church to guide her in things relating to the great concerns of their souls. There are undoubtedly sufficient marks given to guide the children of God in this great affair of judging spirits. Without sufficient marks, the Church would lie open to woeful delusion. And without remedy, she would be open to attack and destruction by her enemies. We need not be afraid to trust these rules. Without a doubt, that Spirit who wrote the Scriptures knew how to give us good rules by which to distinguish His work from all that falsely pretends to be from Him. And this, as I observed before, the Spirit of God has here done deliberately and adequately. Therefore, in my present discussion I confine myself to 1 John, chapter 4 for rules or marks for the trial of spirits.

But before I proceed particularly to speak of these, I would prepare my way by first observing "Indifferent Signs: Elements That Are Neither Sure Signs of the Spirit Nor Marks of the Flesh or the Devil."

INDIFFERENT SIGNS:

Elements That Are Neither Sure Signs of the Spirit
Nor Marks of the Flesh or the Devil

I. It Is Carried on in an Unusual and Extraordinary Way

The work is carried on in an unusual and extraordinary way—provided the variety of difference may still be understood within the limits of Scripture's rules. What the church is accustomed to is not a rule by which we are to judge. There may be new and extraordinary works of God. He has previously acted in an obviously unusual manner. He has brought to pass new things, strange works, and has worked in such a way as to surprise both men and angels. And as God has done thus in times past, so we have no reason to think but that He will do so still. The prophecies of Scripture give us reason to think that God has things to accomplish that have never yet been seen. The Holy Spirit is sovereign in His operation. We know that He uses a great variety. We cannot tell how great a variety He may use within the boundary of the rules He Himself has fixed. We ought not to limit God where He has not limited Himself.

> **We ought not to limit God where He has not limited Himself.**

Therefore, it is not reasonable to determine that a work is

not from God's Holy Spirit because of the extraordinary degree in which the minds of persons are influenced. People may seem to have an extraordinary conviction of the dreadful nature of sin and a very uncommon sense of the misery of a Christless condition. They may have extraordinary views of the certainty and glory of divine things. They may be moved with very extraordinary emotions of fear and sorrow, desire, love, or joy. People may be changed very suddenly and the work be carried on with very unusual swiftness. The persons affected may be very numerous. Many of them may be very young. There may be other unusual circumstances that do not infringe upon Scripture's marks of a work of the Spirit. These things are no argument that the work is not of the Spirit of God.

If in its nature an operation conforms to the rules and marks given in Scripture, the extraordinary and unusual degree of influence and power is rather an argument in its favor. The higher the degree of agreement to the rule, the more evident that conformity. When things are in small degrees, though they be really agreeable to the rule, it is not so easily seen whether their nature agrees with the rule.

There is a great ability in persons to doubt strange things. Elderly persons especially think that for something to be right they must be used to it. They must have heard of it in the days of their fathers. But if this is a good argument—that unusual work is not from the Spirit of God—then the argument was also valid in the apostles' days. In very many respects, the work of the Spirit then was carried on in a manner that never had been seen or heard since the world began. The work was then carried on with more visible and remarkable power than ever. No one had ever seen such mighty and wonderful effects of the Spirit of God. He made sudden changes. He inspired great involvement and zeal in great multitudes. This sudden transformation could be seen in towns, cities, and countries. The progress was swift. The influence of the work was vast. Many other extraordinary circumstances might be mentioned. The great unusual nature of the work surprised the Jews. They knew not what to make of it but could not believe it to be the work of God. Many looked upon the persons that were the subjects of it as bereft of reason.[1]

Prophecy in Scripture describes the beginning of the last and greatest outpouring of the Spirit of God. It is to be in the latter ages of the world. The manner of this work will be very extraordinary and such as never has been seen before. There shall be occasion then to say, "Who has ever heard of such a thing? Who has ever seen such things? Can a country be born in a day or a nation be brought forth in a moment? Yet no sooner is Zion in labor than she gives birth to her children."[2] It may be reasonably expected that the extraordinary manner of the work then will be in proportion to the very extraordinary events. God will bring to pass glorious change in the state of the world.

II. Involuntary Bodily Movement May Occur

A work is not to be judged by any effects on the bodies of men; such as tears, trembling, groans, loud outcries, agonies of body, or the failing of bodily strength. The influence persons are under is not to be judged one way or the other by such effects on the body. Scripture nowhere gives us any such rule. We cannot conclude that persons are under the influence of the true Spirit because we see such effects upon their bodies. This is not given as a mark of the true Spirit; nor on the other hand have we any reason to conclude from any such outward appearances that persons are not under the influence of the Spirit of God. There is no rule of Scripture given us by which to judge spirits that either expressly or indirectly excludes such effects on the body, nor does reason exclude them.

Physical reactions are easily accounted for. Consider the nature of divine and eternal things, the nature of man, and the laws of the union between soul and body. A right influence gives a true and proper sense of things. Consider how this should affect the body. Sometimes the effect is most extraordinary, such as taking away the bodily strength or throwing the body into great agonies and extorting loud outcries. We all suppose and would be ready at any time to say that the misery of hell is dreadful and eternity vast. If a person should have a clear grasp of that misery as it is, it would be more than his feeble frame could bear. This is especially true if at the same time he saw himself in great danger of it and to be utterly uncertain whether he should be delivered from it or to have no security from it one day or hour. Consider human nature. Is it any wonder that when persons have a great sense of that which is so amazingly dreadful, and also have a great view of their own wickedness and God's anger, that things seem to them to promise speedy and immediate destruction? We see the nature of man to be such that when he is greatly exposed to the danger of some terrible calamity, he is always ready to think that now it is coming. When persons' hearts are full of fear in time of war, they are ready to tremble at the shaking of a leaf. They expect the enemy every minute. They say within themselves, "Now I shall be slain."

Suppose that a person saw himself hanging over a great pit full of fierce and glowing flames. He hangs by a thread that he knows to be very weak and not sufficient to bear his weight. He knows that multitudes had been in such circumstances before, and that most of them had fallen and perished. He sees nothing within reach that he can take hold of to save himself. What distress would he be in! How ready to think that now the thread was breaking, that now, this minute, he should be swallowed up in those dreadful flames! And would not he be ready to cry out in such circumstances? How much more those that see themselves in this manner hanging over an infinitely more dreadful pit, or held over it in the hand of God, who at the same time they seem to be exceedingly provoked! No wonder that the wrath of God, when manifested but a little to the soul, overbears human strength.

So it may easily be accounted for that a true sense of the glorious excellency of the Lord Jesus Christ and of His wonderful dying love, and the exercise of a truly spiritual love and joy, should overcome bodily strength. No man can see God and live. Seeing God is but a very small part of fully grasping the glory and love of Christ that the saints enjoy in heaven. Such glory is more than our present frame can bear. Therefore, it is not at all strange that God should sometimes give His saints such foretastes of heaven as to diminish their bodily strength. It was not surprising that the queen of Sheba fainted. Her bodily strength fled away when she saw the glory of Solomon.[3] The Church is the antitype[4] of the queen of Sheba. She is brought, as it were, from the utmost ends of the earth, from being an alien and stranger, far-off, in a state of sin and misery. It should not surprise us that the Church faints when she comes to see the glory of Christ, who is the antitype of Solomon. And especially will the Church be overwhelmed in that prosperous, peaceful, glorious kingdom that He will set up in the world's latter age.

Some object against such extraordinary demonstrations. They say that we have no instances of them recorded in the New Testament under the extraordinary outpourings of the Spirit. Scripture is silent, but I can see no force in the objection since neither reason nor any rule of Scripture exclude such things, especially considering what was observed under the previous paragraph. I do not know that we have any specific mention in the New Testament of any person's weeping or groaning or sighing through fear of hell or awareness of God's anger. But is there anybody so foolish as to argue from this that when these things appear in anyone, their convictions are not from the Spirit of God? We do not argue thus for two good reasons. First, we know the nature of man. And second, the Scripture informs us concerning the nature of eternal things and the nature of the convictions of God's Spirit. Therefore, there is no need that anything should be said in particular concerning these eternal, incidental effects. Nobody supposes that there is any need of specific Scripture for every external, accidental manifestation of the inward activity of the mind. Such circumstances are not particularly recorded in sacred history. But from the general accounts we have, it is reasonable to think that such things must have occurred in those days. And there is also reason to think that such a great outpouring of the Spirit was not wholly without those more extraordinary effects on persons' bodies.

The Philippian jailer, in particular, seems to have been an instance of that nature when he, in the utmost distress and amazement, came trembling and fell down before Paul and Silas. His falling down then does not seem to be a matter of putting himself into a posture of supplication or humble address to Paul and Silas. He seems not to have said anything to them then, but he first brought them out and then said to them, "Sirs, what must I do to be saved?"[5] His falling down seems to be from the same cause as his trembling.

The psalmist gives an account of his crying aloud and the great weakening of his body under convictions of conscience and a sense of the guilt of sin. "When I kept silent, my bones wasted away through my groaning all the day long. For day and night your hand was heavy upon me; my strength was sapped as in the heat of summer" (Psalm 32:3-4). We may at least argue from this that a conviction of sin may in some cases produce similar effects. The psalmist would not represent his case by what would be absurd.

We read that when the disciples saw Christ coming to them in the storm, they took Him for some terrible enemy, threatening their destruction in that storm. "They . . . cried out in fear."[6] Why then should it be thought strange that persons would cry out for fear when God appears to them as a terrible enemy and they see themselves in great danger of being swallowed up in the bottomless gulf of eternal misery? The spouse in the Song of Solomon twice speaks of herself as overpowered with the love of Christ. Her body becomes weak, and she faints.[7] From this we may at least argue that a similar effect may well arise from such a cause in the saints. Such an effect will sometimes be seen in the church of Christ.

It is a weak objection that the insights of enthusiasts have a great effect on their bodies. The Quakers used to tremble. This is no argument that Saul (afterwards Paul) and the jailer did not tremble from real convictions of conscience. Indeed, all such objections from effects on the body, let them be greater or less, seem to be very silly. They who argue in this manner proceed in the dark. They know not what ground they go upon, nor by what rule they judge. The root and course of things are to be looked at. The nature of the operations and affections are to be inquired into and examined by the rule of God's Word and not by the actions of mere sensual spirits.

III. It Produces Much Talk About the Christian Faith

It is no argument that an operation on the minds of people is not the work of the Spirit of God because it produces much talk about the Christian faith. True Christian faith is always contrary to the nature of the Pharisees, which was showy and delighted in men's applause. Such is human nature that it is morally impossible that there should be a great concern, strong affection, and general engagement of mind among a people without causing a notable, visible, and open commotion and alteration among that people. Surely it is no argument that the minds of persons are not under the influence of God's Spirit because they are very much moved. Indeed, spiritual and eternal things are so great and of such infinite concern that there is a great absurdity in men's being but moderately moved and affected by them. Surely it is no argument that they are not moved by the Spirit of God, that they are affected with these things in some measure as they deserve or in some proportion to their importance. Since time began, when did people who were greatly affected by any matter not talk much about it or make a stir? The nature of man will not allow it.

Indeed, Christ says, "The kingdom of God comes not with observation."[8] That is, it will not consist of what is outward and visible. It will not be like earthly kingdoms, set up with outward pomp in some particular place that shall be especially the royal city and seat of the kingdom. Christ explains Himself: "Nor will people say, 'Here it is,' or 'There it is,' because the kingdom of God is within you."[9] The kingdom of God will not be set up in the world on the ruin of Satan's kingdom without a very observable, great effect. There will be a mighty change in the state of things. The whole world will observe it with astonishment. Such an effect as this is held forth in the prophecies of Scripture and by Christ Himself. In this very place and even in His own explanation of these previous words, Jesus says, "For the Son of Man in His day will be like the lightning, which flashes and lights up the sky from one end to the other."[10] This is to distinguish Christ's coming to set up His kingdom from the coming of false christs. He tells us the false christs will come in a private manner in the deserts and in the secret chambers. But the setting up of the kingdom of God will be open and public, in the sight of the whole world, with clear manifestation. It will be like lightning that cannot be hid but glares in everyone's eyes and shines from one side of heaven to the other. We find that when Christ's kingdom came by that remarkable pouring out of the Spirit in the apostles' days, it caused a great stir everywhere. What a mighty opposition there was in Jerusalem on the occasion of that great outpouring of the Spirit! And so it was in Samaria, Antioch, Ephesus, Corinth, and other places! The affair filled the world with noise and gave occasion to some to say of the apostles that they had turned the world upside-down.[11]

IV. Intense Religious Emotions Are Present

It is no argument that an operation on the minds of people is not the work of the Spirit of God because many who are the subjects of it have great impressions made on their emotions. People have many impressions on their emotions. This does not prove that they have nothing else. It is easy to account for the fact that people of all kinds have their minds engaged with intense thought and strong affections about invisible things. Yes, it would be strange if this were not so. Such is our nature that we cannot think of things invisible without a degree of emotion. I challenge any thinking person to fix his thoughts on God or Christ or the things of another world without imaginary ideas attending his meditations. The more engaged the mind is and the more intense the thoughtful observation and passion, still the more lively and strong the imaginary idea will ordinarily be. This is especially true when attended with surprise. And this is the case when the mental prospect is very new and takes strong hold of emotions like fear or joy.

It is also the case when the change of the state and views of the mind is sudden from a contrary extreme, as from that which was extremely dreadful to that which is extremely ravishing and delightful. And it is no wonder that many persons do not distinguish well between that which is imaginary and that which is intellectual and spiritual. It is not surprising that they may put too much weight on the imaginary part and be eager to speak of it in the account they give of their experience. This is especially so of persons with less understanding and ability to discern.

God has given us the faculty of emotion. He has so made us that we cannot think of things spiritual and invisible without some exercise of this faculty. Therefore, it appears to me that such is our state and nature that this faculty serves and helps the other faculties of the mind when a proper use is made of it. Emotion is helpful in spite of the fact that often it is too strong and the other faculties weak. Often emotion dominates and disturbs them in their exercise. It appears to me from many instances with which I am familiar that God has really made use of emotion for truly divine purposes. This is especially true in some who are not highly educated. God seems to condescend to their circumstances. He deals with them as babes. As He instructed His Church while in a state of ignorance and minority by types[12] and outward representations, so He instructs them. I can see nothing unreasonable in such a position. Let others who frequently deal with souls about spiritual concerns judge whether experience does not confirm this.

Ecstasy is no argument that a work is not of the Spirit of God. Some people have been carried beyond themselves. They have had their minds transported into a course of strong and pleasing emotions. They have a kind of vision as though they were snatched up even to heaven and there saw glorious sights. I have been acquainted with some such instances. And I see no need of bringing the help of the devil into the account that we give of these things. Nor yet do I suppose them to be of the same nature with the visions of the prophets or Saint Paul's rapture into paradise. Human nature, under these exercises and emotions, is all that need be brought into the account. We have already discussed the fact that persons may be under a true sense of a glorious and wonderful greatness and excellency of divine things. They may have soul-ravishing views of the beauty and love of Christ. And they might have their normal strength overpowered. Therefore, it is not at all strange that with so many affected in this manner, there should be some people of a particular makeup who would have their emotions thus affected. The same effect bears a proportion and analogy to other effects of the strong exercise of their minds. When the thoughts are so fixed, when the emotions are so strong, when the whole soul is so engaged, ravished, and swallowed up, it is no wonder that all other parts of the body are so affected as to lose their strength. It is no wonder that the whole frame is ready to dissolve. We know intense contemplation and especially exercises of mind affect the brain in particular (especially in some temperaments). Is it any wonder that in such a case the brain is affected? Is it surprising that its strength and spirits for a time are diverted from impressions made on the organs of external sense? It is not surprising that the brain may be wholly employed in a course of pleasing, delightful emotions corresponding with the present frame of the mind.

Some are ready to interpret such things improperly. They lay too much weight on them as prophetic visions, divine revelations. In some instances I have known the issue to be otherwise. Yet it appears to me that such things are evidently sometimes from the Spirit of God, though indirectly. That is, people's extraordinary frame of mind, and that strong and lively sense of divine things that is the occasion of this frame of mind, is from His Spirit. And the mind continues in its holy frame and retains a divine sense of the excellency of spiritual things even in its rapture. This holy frame and sense is from the Spirit of God, though the emotions that attend it are but accidental. Therefore, there is usually something or other in them that is confused, improper, and false.

V. Example Is a Great Means

It is God's manner to use means in carrying on His work in the world. It is no more an argument against the divine origin of the effect that example is used than if it was by any other means. Scripture teaches that people should be influenced by one another's good example. The Scripture directs us to set good examples to that end[13] and also directs us to be influenced by the good examples of others and to follow them.[14] Thus it appears that example is one of God's means. Certainly it is no argument that a work is not of God because His own means are used to effect it.

An example is a scriptural way of carrying on God's work, and so it is a reasonable way. It is no argument that example rather than reason influences men. When people, by example, hold forth truth to one another, this tends to enlighten the mind and to convince reason. All agree it is reasonable to signify things to one another by words to enlighten each other's minds. But the same thing may be expressed more fully and effectively by actions. Words are of use only as they convey our own ideas to others. There is a language in actions. And in some cases the language of action is much more clear and convincing than words. Therefore, persons who are greatly affected by the example of others are no argument against the goodness of the effect, even though only seeing the tokens of great and extraordinary affection in the behavior of others makes the impression.

> **There is a language in actions. And in some cases the language of action is much more clear and convincing than words.**

We may take for granted what they are experiencing without hearing them say one word. There may be language enough in their behavior to convey their minds to others. Their behavior shows how they see things more than words alone can possibly do. Suppose you see someone suffering extreme physical torment. You receive clearer ideas and more convincing evidence of what he is suffering by his actions than you could by the words alone of an unaffected, indifferent person describing his suffering. Likewise, you get a better idea of things excellent and delightful from the behavior of one who is actually experiencing them. The dull narration of one who is inexperienced and insensitive cannot match this.

I desire that this matter may be examined by the strictest reason. Weak and ignorant people are much influenced by example, but also those who make the greatest boast of strength of reason are more influenced by reason held forth through example than almost any other way. Therefore, is it not apparent that effects produced in persons' minds by example are rational? Now, the religious emotions of many, when raised by example, whether by hearing the Word preached or any other means, may prove fleshy and soon vanish. They are like those Christ represents as the stony-ground hearers. But the emotions of some thus moved by example are abiding and prove to result in salvation.

There never yet was a time of remarkable pouring out of the Spirit and great revival of the Christian faith but that example had a main hand. So it was at the Reformation and in the apostles' days in Jerusalem and Samaria and Ephesus and other parts of the world. This is obvious to anyone who examines the account we have in the Acts of the apostles. As in those days one person was moved by another, so one city or town was influenced by the example of another.[15]

It is no valid objection against examples being so much used that the Scripture speaks of the word as the principal means of carrying on God's work. The word of God is the principal means by which other means operate and are made effectual. Even the sacraments have no effect but by the word. And so it is that example becomes effective. For all that is visible to the eye is vague and vain without the word of God to instruct and guide the mind. It is the word of God that is indeed held forth and applied by example, just as the word of the Lord sounded forth to other towns in Macedonia and Achaia by the example of those who believed in Thessalonica.[16]

Example should be a great means of helping the church of God to grow. This is expressed in many ways in Scripture. Ruth following Naomi out of the land of Moab into the land of Israel expresses example.[17] Ruth resolved that she would not leave Naomi but would go wherever she went, lodging where she lodged. Naomi's people would be her people and Naomi's God her God. Ruth was the ancestral mother of David and of Christ. She was undoubtedly a great type of the Church, upon which account her history is inserted in the canon of Scripture. Ruth left the land of Moab and its gods. She came to put her trust under the shadow of the wings of the God of Israel.[18] In this we have a type of the conversion not only of the Gentile Church, but also of every sinner, who is naturally an alien and stranger. In his conversion he forgets his own people and father's house, becoming a fellow citizen with the saints. He becomes a true Israelite.

The Church's growing by use of example is also expressed in the effect of the spouse in the Song of Solomon on the daughters of Jerusalem when she was sick with love.[19] This test refers to the Spirit and the bride. It pictures visible Christians who are first awakened by seeing the spouse (Christ) in such extraordinary circumstances. Then they are converted. This is undoubtedly one way that "the Spirit and the bride say, 'Come.'"[20]

It is foretold that the work of God will be very much carried on by means of example in the last great outpouring of the Spirit. This last great outpouring of the Spirit will introduce the glorious day of the church, so often spoken of in Scripture.

> *"The inhabitants of one city will go to another and say, 'Let us go at once to entreat the LORD and seek the LORD Almighty. I myself am going.' And many peoples and powerful nations will come to Jerusalem to seek the LORD Almighty and to entreat him." This is what the LORD Almighty says: "In those days ten men from all languages and nations will take firm hold of one Jew by the hem of his robe and say, 'Let us go with you because we have heard that God is with you.'"[21]*

VI. *Subjects of It Are Guilty of Rash Acts and Unconventional Conduct*

It is no sign that a work is not from the Spirit of God when many who seem to be the subjects of it are guilty of great rash acts and unconventional conduct. The end for which God pours out His Spirit is to make men holy, and not to make them politicians. It is no wonder that in a mixed multitude of all sorts—wise and unwise, young and old, with weak and strong natural abilities, under strong impressions of mind—there are many who behave rashly. Few know how to conduct themselves under intense emotion of any kind, whether of a temporal or spiritual nature. To do so requires a great deal of discretion, strength, and steadiness of mind. A thousand rash acts will not prove a work is not of the Spirit of God. If there are not only rash acts, but also many things that are unconventional and really contrary to the rules of God's holy Word, it still does not mean that a work is not from God. This can be accounted for from the extreme weakness of human nature. It is also explained by the remaining darkness and corruption of people who have a real zeal for God but are yet to be the subjects of the saving influences of God's Spirit.

The end for which God pours out His Spirit is to make men holy, and not to make them politicians.

We have a remarkable instance of this in the New Testament—the church at Corinth. There the people shared the abundant outpouring of the Spirit in the apostles' days. However, among them abounded unconventional and rash acts. Scarcely any church is more celebrated than the Corinthian one for being blessed with large measures of the Spirit of God. This blessing included the Spirit's ordinary influences in convincing and converting sinners. It also included the Spirit's extraordinary and miraculous gifts. In spite of the Spirit's blessing, there were many rash acts—great and sinful irregularities, strange confusion at the Lord's Supper and in the exercise of church discipline. To all this may be added those believers' indecent manner of attending other parts of public worship, their bickering and contention about their teachers, and even the exercise of their extraordinary gifts of prophecy, speaking with tongues, and the like, wherein they spoke and acted by the immediate inspiration of the Spirit of God.

If we see great rash acts and even sinful irregularities in some who are great instruments for carrying on the work, it will not prove it *not* to be the work of God. The apostle Peter was a great, eminently holy, and inspired apostle. He was one of the chief instruments of setting up the Christian church in the world. Yet when he was actually engaged in this work, he was guilty of a great and sinful error in his conduct. The apostle Paul speaks of this: "When Peter came to Antioch, I opposed him to his face because he was in the wrong. Before certain men came from James, he used to eat with the Gentiles. But when they arrived, he began to draw back and separate himself from the Gentiles because he was afraid of those who belonged to the circumcision group. The other Jews joined him in his hypocrisy, so that by their hypocrisy even Barnabas was led astray."[22] Next to Christ, Peter was one of the chief of those who were the very foundation on which the whole church was built. Lesser instruments do not have the extraordinary ministry of the divine Spirit that Peter had.

If a great pillar of the Christian church was guilty of such an irregularity, is it any wonder if other, lesser instruments should be guilty of many irregularities?

Many who are the subjects or the instruments of a work are guilty of too much bold self-confidence. They even censure others as unconverted. But this is no evidence that a work is not of God. Their self-confidence may appear in mistakes they have embraced concerning the marks by which they are to judge the hypocrisy and carnality of others. Or they may not be making due allowance for the infirmity and corruption that is left in the hearts of the saints. In addition, they may lack a clear sense of their own blindness and weakness. They do not see their remaining corruption. Therefore, spiritual pride may have a secret expression in this way. It is disguised and not easily discovered.

Truly pious people may have a great deal of remaining blindness and corruption. And they may be liable to make mistakes about the marks of hypocrisy. Undoubtedly, all will allow this, and it is not hard to believe that pious people should sometimes fall into such errors as these. It is easy to understand that the remaining corruption of good men would sometimes have an unobserved vent in this way rather than in most other ways. Without doubt (however sad), many holy men have erred because of their remaining blindness and corruption.

Lukewarmness in the Christian faith is vile, and zeal an excellent grace; yet above all other Christian virtues, this needs to be strictly watched and searched. For it is zeal with which corruption and pride and human passion is very apt to mix unobserved. This happens every time great reformation seeks a revival of zeal in the Church of God. With each reformation there have been things that did not conform to social convention. In some notable cases, these developed into an undue strict adherence to rigorous standards. Thus in the apostles' days a great deal of zeal was expressed concerning unclean meats. With heated spirits Christians condemned and censured others as not true Christians. The apostle acknowledged that both could be influenced by a spirit of real piety: "He who eats meat, eats to the Lord, for he give thanks to God; and he who abstains, does so to the Lord and gives thanks to God" (Romans 14:6).

Later, when Christianity was still greatly flourishing, there was a spirit of eminent holiness and zeal prevailing in the Church. Then the zeal of Christians was expressed in a very improper and undue severity. This time zeal was in the exercise of church discipline toward delinquents. In some cases they would not admit them into their love and communion though they appeared humble and penitent. And in the days of Constantine the Great, the zeal of Christians against the heathen became persecution. The Reforma-tion was a glorious revival of the Christian faith. Yet at this time zeal in many instances became improper severity. Sometimes zeal turned into a degree of persecution in some of the best-known reformers, as in the great Calvin. And many in those days were guilty of severely censuring others who differed from them in some points of theology.

VII. Errors in Judgment and Delusions of Satan Intermix with the Work

Nor are many errors in judgment and some delusions of Satan intermixed with the work any argument that the work in general is not of the Spirit of God. However great a spiritual influence may be, it is not to be expected that the Spirit of God should be given now in the same manner as it was to the apostles. The Spirit, without error, guided the apostles in points of Christian doctrine. Therefore, what they taught can be relied on as a rule to the Christian church.

And if many delusions of Satan appear at the same time that a great religious concern prevails, it is not an argument that the work in general is not the work of God. In Egypt there were true miracles wrought by the hand of God in spite of the fact that Jannes and Jambres wrought false miracles at the same time by the hand of the devil.[23] Yes, the same persons may experience great influences of the Spirit of God and yet in some things be led away by the delusions of Satan. This is no more a paradox than many other things that are true of real saints. In the present state, grace dwells with so much corruption.

The new man and the old man subsist together in the same person. The kingdom of God and the kingdom of the devil remain for a while together in the same heart. Many godly persons have undoubtedly in the present and previous ages exposed themselves to woeful delusions. They have an aptness to put too much weight on impulses and impressions. They treat these impulses and impressions as if they were immediate revelations from God to signify something future or to direct them where to go and what to do.

VIII. Some Fall Away into Gross Errors or Scandalous Practices

If it appears that God has done a special work in someone and then that person falls away into gross errors or scandalous practices, that is no argument that the work in general is not the work of the Spirit of God. That there are some counterfeits is not an argument that nothing is true. Such things are always expected in a time of reformation. Every great revival of the Christian faith has been attended with many such things. Instances of this nature in the apostles' days were too numerous to be counted. Some believers fell away into gross heresies. Others fell into vile practices. They seemed to be the subjects of a work of the Spirit. They were accepted for a while as brethren and companions among those who were truly so and were not suspected until they went out from them. And some of these were teachers and officers—eminent persons in the Christian Church, whom God had endowed with miraculous gifts of the Holy Spirit, as appears in the beginning of the sixth chapter of Hebrews.

That there are some counterfeits is not an argument that nothing is true.

An example of these was Judas, one of the twelve apostles. He had long been constantly united to and intimately conversant with a company of truly experienced disciples. He was not discovered or suspected until he revealed himself by his scandalous practice. Jesus Himself in all external things had treated him as if he had truly been a disciple. Jesus even invested him with the office of apostle, sending him forth to preach the Gospel and endowing him with miraculous gifts of the Spirit. For though Christ knew Judas, yet Christ did not then clothe himself with the character of all-knowing Judge and Searcher of Hearts. Christ acted the part of a minister of the visible Church (for He was His Father's minister). And therefore Christ did not reject Judas until he had revealed himself by his scandalous practice. This gives an example to guides and rulers of the visible Church. They are not to take it upon themselves to act the part of Searcher of Hearts but are to be influenced in their governing by what is visible and open. There were some instances then of apostates who were esteemed eminently full of the grace of God's Spirit.

An instance of this nature probably was Nicolas, one of the seven deacons. He was looked upon by the Christians in Jerusalem, in the time of that extraordinary pouring out of the Spirit, as a man full of the Holy Spirit. For that reason he was chosen out of the multitudes of Christians to that office.[24] Yet he afterwards fell away and became the head of a sect of vile heretics with gross practices, called from his name the sect of the Nicolaitans.[25]

So it was in the time of the reformation from popery. How great was the number of those who for a while seemed to join with the reformers, yet fell away into the grossest and most absurd errors and abominable practices. This falling away is particularly observable in times of great pouring out of the Spirit to revive the Christian faith in the world. A number of those who for a while seemed to partake in it have fallen off into whimsical and extravagant errors and gross enthusiasm. They boast of high degrees of spirituality and perfection, censuring and condemning others as carnal. Thus it was with the Gnostics[26] in the apostles' times. And thus it was with several sects at the Reformation. As Anthony Burgess observes:

> The first worthy reformers and glorious instruments of God found a bitter conflict. They were exercised not only

with formalists and traditional papists but also men that pretended themselves to be more enlightened than the reformers. The formalists, traditionalists, and pretenders called those that adhered to the Scripture Literists and Vowelists. These terms of derision implied that they were concerned with the words and vowels of the Scripture, but totally ignored the Spirit of God. Wherever the true doctrine of the Gospel broke forth to displace popery, soon such opinions arose like tares that came up among the good wheat. Great divisions were raised and the reformation was made abominable and odious to the world. It was as if the reformation had been the sun to give heat and warmth to those worms and serpents to crawl out of the ground. Hence they criticized Luther and said he had only preached a carnal Gospel.[27]

Some leaders of those wild enthusiasts were for a while highly esteemed by the first reformers and particularly dear to them. In England, when vital Christian faith prospered in the days of King Charles I and Oliver Cromwell, such things as these abounded. And so in New England, in her purest days when vital piety flourished, such kinds of things as these broke out. Therefore, the devil's sowing of such tares is no proof that a true work of the Spirit of God is not gloriously carried on.

IX. Ministers Promote It by the Terrors of God's Holy Law

It is no argument that a work is not from the Spirit of God because ministers seem to promote it by insisting on the terrors of God's holy law. And they promote this work with a great deal of pathos and earnestness. It is generally supposed there is a real hell of dreadful and never-ending torments. Multitudes are in great danger of this hell. The greater part of people in Christian countries do actually fall into this hell from generation to generation. They fall for lack of a sense of its dread and for lack of taking due care to avoid it. Then why is it not proper for those who have the care of souls to take great pains to make men aware of it? Why should they not be told as much of the truth as can be? If I am in danger of going to hell, I would be glad to know as much as I possibly can of the terror of it. If I am very prone to neglect proper care to avoid hell, who does me the best kindness? He who does most to represent the truth of the case or he that sets forth my misery and danger in the liveliest manner? I appeal to all. Is this not the course they would take in case of exposure to any great physical calamity?

Suppose any of you who are parents saw one of your children in a house on fire and in imminent danger of being consumed in the flames. If the child were oblivious of his danger and neglected to escape after you had often called to him, would you go on to speak to him only in a cold and indifferent manner? Would not you cry aloud and call earnestly to him? Would you not represent the danger he was in and his own folly in delaying? Would you not do this in the most lively manner of which you were capable? Does not nature itself teach this and oblige you to it? If you continue to speak only in a normal manner, would not the people around you think you lacked reason? This is not the way of mankind in physical affairs of great significance that require earnest attention and quick action and about which they are greatly concerned. They will not warn them only once or in a cold and indifferent manner. Nature teaches us otherwise.

Do we who have the care of souls know what hell is? Have we seen the state of the damned? Are we aware how dreadful their case is? Do we know that most people go there unaware of their danger? And do we see that our hearers are not aware of their danger? If we knew all this, it would be morally impossible for us to avoid passionately telling them the dreadfulness of that misery and their great exposure to it. We would cry aloud to them!

> **When ministers preach about hell and warn sinners to avoid it in a cold manner—though they may say in words that it is infinitely terrible—they contradict themselves. For actions, as I observed before, have a language as well as words.**

When ministers preach about hell and warn sinners to avoid it in a cold manner—though they may say in words that it is infinitely terrible—they contradict themselves. For actions, as I observed before, have a language as well as words. If a preacher's words represent the sinner's state as infinitely dreadful while his behavior and manner of speaking contradict it—showing that the preacher does not think so—he defeats his own purpose. The language of his actions in such a case is much more powerful than the bare meaning of his words. Not that I think only the law should be preached. The Gospel is to be preached as well as the law. The law is to be preached only to make way for the Gospel, and in order that it may be preached more powerfully. The main work of a minister is to preach the Gospel. "Christ is the end of the law so that there may be righteousness for everyone who believes."[28] A minister misses his calling very much if he insists so much on the terrors of the law as to forget his Lord and neglects to preach the Gospel. And yet the law must be insisted on, and the preaching of the Gospel will be in vain without it.

Some say it is unreasonable to frighten people into heaven. But I think it is reasonable to try to frighten people away from hell.

Such earnestness and affection in speaking is beautiful because of the nature and importance of the subject. Preachers may be improperly loud. Their noisy and undisciplined manner of speaking does not naturally arise from the nature of the subject. In these cases the content of the message and the manner of delivery do not agree. Some say it is unreasonable to frighten people into heaven. But I think it is reasonable to try to frighten people away from hell. They stand upon its brink and are about to fall into it and are unaware of their danger. Is it not a reasonable thing to frighten a person out of a house on fire? The word *frighten* is commonly used for sudden, unreasonable fear or groundless surprise. But surely a just fear, for which there is good reason, is not to be spoken against under any such name.

FOOTNOTES TO THIS SECTION

1. "Others mocking said, 'They are full of new wine'" (Acts 2:13, NKJV). "Now as he thus made his defense, Festus said with a loud voice, 'Paul, you are beside yourself! Much learning is driving you mad!'" (Acts 26:24, NKJV). "We are fools for Christ's sake, but you are wise in Christ! We are weak, but you are strong! You are distinguished, but we are dishonored!" (1 Corinthians 4:10, NKJV).

2. Isaiah 66:8.

3. "And when the queen of Sheba had seen all the wisdom of Solomon, the house that he had built, the food on his table, the seating of his servants,

the service of his waiters and their apparel, his cupbearers, and his entryway by which he went up to the house of the LORD, there was no more spirit in her" (1 Kings 10:4, NKJV).

4. An antitype is the New Testament embodiment of truth pictured in shadowy form on the pages of Old Testament history as a type.

5. "Then he called for a light, ran in, and fell down trembling before Paul and Silas. And he brought them out and said, 'Sirs, what must I do to be saved?'" (Acts 16:29-30, NKJV).

6. "And when the disciples saw Him walking on the sea, they were troubled, saying, 'It is a ghost!' And they cried out for fear" (Matthew 14:26, NKJV).

7. "Stay me with flagons, comfort me with apples: for I am sick with love." And again, "O daughters of Jerusalem, I charge you—if you find my lover, what will you tell him? Tell him I am faint with love" (Song of Solomon 2:5, KJV; 5:8).

8. Luke 17:20, NKJV.

9. Luke 17:21.

10. Luke 17:24.

11. "But when they did not find them, they dragged Jason and some brethren to the rulers of the city, crying out, 'These who have turned the world upside down have come here too'" (Acts 17:6, NKJV).

12. A type is a shadow cast on the pages of Old Testament history by a truth whose full embodiment, or antitype, is found in New Testament revelation.

13. "In the same way, let your light shine before men, that they may see your good deeds and praise your Father in heaven" (Matthew 5:16). "Wives, in the same way be submissive to your husbands so that, if any of them do not believe the word, they may be won over without words by the behavior of their wives" (1 Peter 3:1). "Don't let anyone look down on you because you are young, but set an example for the believers in speech, in life, in love, in faith and in purity" (1 Timothy 4:12). "In everything set them an example by doing what is good. In your teaching show integrity, seriousness" (Titus 2:7).

14. "Now about food sacrificed to idols: We know that we all possess knowledge. Knowledge puffs up, but love builds up. The man who thinks he knows something does not yet know as he ought to know. But the man who loves God is known by God. So then, about eating food sacrificed to idols: We know that an idol is nothing at all in the world and that there is no God but one. For even if there are so-called gods, whether in heaven or on earth (as indeed, there are many 'gods' and many 'lords'), yet for us there is but one God, the Father, from whom all things came and for whom we live; and there is but one Lord, Jesus Christ, through whom all things came and through whom we live. But not everyone knows this. Some people are still so accustomed to idols that when they eat such food they think of it as having been sacrificed to an idol, and since their conscience is weak, it is defiled" (1 Corinthians 8:1-7). "We do not want you to become lazy, but to imitate those who through faith and patience inherit what has been promised" (Hebrews 6:12). "Join with others in following my example,

brothers, and take note of those who live according to the pattern we gave you" (Philippians 3:17). "Therefore we do not lose heart. Though outwardly we are wasting away, yet inwardly we are being renewed day by day" (2 Corinthians 4:16). "I hope you will put up with a little of my foolishness; but you are already doing that. I am jealous for you with a godly jealousy. I promised you to one husband, to Christ, so that I might present you as a pure virgin to him" (2 Corinthians 11:1-2). "We did this, not because we do not have the right to such help, but in order to make ourselves a model for you to follow" (2 Thessalonians 3:9). "And so you became a model to all the believers in Macedonia and Achaia" (1 Thessalonians 1:7).

15. "And so you became a model to all the believers in Macedonia and Achaia. The Lord's message rang out from you not only in Macedonia and Achaia—your faith in God has become known everywhere. Therefore we do not need to say anything about it" (1 Thessalonians 1:7-8).

16. "You became imitators of us and of the Lord; in spite of severe suffering, you welcomed the message with the joy given by the Holy Spirit. And so you became a model to all the believers in Macedonia and Achaia. The Lord's message rang out from you not only in Macedonia and Achaia—your faith in God has become known everywhere. Therefore we do not need to say anything about it" (1 Thessalonians 1:6-8).

17. Ruth 1:16-17.

18. "May the LORD repay you for what you have done. May you be richly rewarded by the LORD, the God of Israel, under whose wings you have come to take refuge" (Ruth 2:12).

19. "O daughters of Jerusalem, I charge you—if you find my lover, what will you tell him? Tell him I am faint with love. How is your beloved better than others, most beautiful of women? How is your beloved better than others, that you charge us so? . . . Where has your lover gone, most beautiful of women? Which way did your lover turn, that we may look for him with you?" (Song of Solomon 5:8-9; 6:1).

20. "The Spirit and the bride say, 'Come!' And let him who hears say, 'Come!' Whoever is thirsty, let him come; and whoever wishes, let him take the free gift of the water of life" (Revelation 22:17).

21. Zechariah 8:21-23.

22. Galatians 2:11-13.

23. "Pharaoh then summoned wise men and sorcerers and the Egyptian magicians also did the same things by their secret arts: Each one threw down his staff and it became a snake. But Aaron's staff swallowed up their staffs. Yet Pharaoh's heart became hard and he would not listen to them, just as the LORD had said. Then the LORD said to Moses, 'Pharaoh's heart is unyielding; he refuses to let the people go. Go to Pharaoh in the morning as he goes out to the water. Wait on the bank of the Nile to meet him, and take in your hand the staff that was changed into a snake. Then say to him, "The LORD, the God of the Hebrews, has sent me to say to you: Let my people go, so that they may worship me in the desert. But until now you have

not listened. This is what the LORD says: By this you will know that I am the LORD: With the staff that is in my hand I will strike the water of the Nile, and it will be changed into blood. The fish in the Nile will die, and the river will stink; the Egyptians will not be able to drink its water."' The LORD said to Moses, 'Tell Aaron, "Take your staff and stretch out your hand over the waters of Egypt—over the streams and canals, over the ponds and all the reservoirs"—and they will turn to blood. Blood will be everywhere in Egypt, even in the wooden buckets and stone jars.' Moses and Aaron did just as the LORD had commanded. He raised his staff in the presence of Pharaoh and his officials and struck the water of the Nile, and all the water was changed into blood. The fish in the Nile died, and the river smelled so bad the Egyptians could not drink its water. Blood was everywhere in Egypt. But the Egyptian magicians did the same things by their secret arts, and Pharaoh's heart became hard; he would not listen to Moses and Aaron, just as the LORD had said" (Exodus 7:11-22). "But Elymas the sorcerer (for that is what his name means) opposed them and tried to turn the proconsul from the faith" (Acts 13:8). "Just as Jannes and Jambres opposed Moses, so also these men oppose the truth—men of depraved minds who, as far as the faith is concerned, are rejected" (2 Timothy 3:8).

24. "Brothers, choose seven men from among you who are known to be full of the Spirit and wisdom. We will turn this responsibility over to them" (Acts 6:3). "This proposal pleased the whole group. They chose Stephen, a man full of faith and of the Holy Spirit; also Philip, Procorus, Nicanor, Timon, Parmenas, and Nicolas from Antioch, a convert to Judaism" (Acts 6:5).

25. "But you have this in your favor: You hate the practices of the Nicolaitans, which I also hate. . . . Likewise you also have those who hold to the teaching of the Nicolaitans" (Revelation 2:6, 15). But though these heretics assumed his name, it does not follow that he countenanced the enormity of their sins. See Nicolas in *Calmet's Dictionary*.

26. *Gnostic* comes from the Greek word *gnosis*, which means "knowledge." Gnostics claimed secret knowledge that could be obtained only by that part of humanity that was spiritual. This elevating of a limited number to a special, privileged class and the consigning of the vast majority to unredeemable destruction was one of its worst features. Matter was utterly and irretrievably evil. The God of the Jews was the Creator, but He was not the Supreme Being. He was an inferior demiurge. The Supreme Bring was unknowable. The problem was how this pure being could relate to the corrupt world. The problem was solved with a series of demiurges called aeons. The historical Christ was only a man, but he was taken possession of by the heavenly Christ who was the brightest of all aeons.

27. *Spiritual Refinings*, Part I, Sermon 23, p. 132.

28. Romans 10:4.

BIBLICAL SIGNS:

Distinguishing Scriptural Evidences of a Work of the Spirit of God

I will now show positively what are the sure, distinguishing scriptural evidences and marks of a work of the Spirit of God. By these marks we may judge any operation we find in ourselves or see among people without danger of being misled. In this I shall confine myself wholly to those marks that are given us by the apostle John. In the fourth chapter of his first epistle, this matter is handled more plainly and fully than anywhere else in the Bible. In speaking to these marks, I shall take them in the order in which I find them in that chapter.

I. The Operation Exalts Jesus

When the operation raises people's esteem of Jesus, it is a sure sign that it is from the Spirit of God. Jesus was born of the Virgin and was crucified outside the gates of Jerusalem. This work of the Spirit of God confirms and establishes people's minds in the truth of what the Gospel declares to us about Jesus being the Son of God and the Savior of men. The apostle gives us this sign in the second and third verses: "This is how you can recognize the Spirit of God: Every spirit that acknowledges that Jesus Christ has come in the flesh is from God, but every spirit that does not acknowledge Jesus is not from God." This implies confessing that there was such a person who appeared in Palestine and suffered those things that are recorded of Him. But it also implies that He was Christ—that is, the Son of God, anointed to be Lord and Savior, as the name Jesus Christ implies. That this much is implied in the apostle's meaning is confirmed by the fifteenth verse where the apostle is still on the same subject of signs of the true Spirit: "If anyone acknowledges that Jesus is the Son of God, God lives in him and he in God." It is to be observed that the word *acknowledge*, as it is often used in the New Testament, signifies more than merely allowing. It implies establishing and confirming a thing by testimony and declaring it with visible esteem and affection. "Whoever acknowledges me before men, I will also acknowledge him before my Father in heaven." "Therefore I will praise [acknowledge] you among the Gentiles; I will sing hymns to your name." And, "every tongue [will] confess [acknowledge] that Jesus Christ is Lord, to the glory of God the Father."[1] This is the force of the expression as the apostle John uses it in this place. John confirms this in the next chapter, verse 1: "Everyone who believes that Jesus is the Christ is born of God, and everyone who loves the father loves his child as well." And in the parallel Scripture of the apostle Paul we have the same rule given to distinguish the true Spirit from all counterfeits: "Therefore I tell you that no one who is speaking by the Spirit of God says, 'Jesus be cursed,' and no one can say, 'Jesus is Lord,' except by the Holy Spirit."[2]

When the Spirit is at work among people, He will plainly convince them of Christ and lead them to Him. He will confirm their minds in the belief of the history of Christ as He appeared in the flesh, the Son of God who was sent by God to save sinners. He will confirm that Christ is the only Savior and that they stand in great need of Him. The Spirit begets in people higher and more honorable thoughts of Christ than they used to have and to incline their emotions more to Him. This plain persuasion about Christ is a sure sign that it is the work of the true and right Spirit. However incapable we may be to determine whether that conviction and affection be saving or not, it is the work of the Holy Spirit.

The words of the apostle are remarkable! The person to whom the Spirit gives testimony and for whom He raises their esteem must be Jesus—the one who appeared in the flesh. No other Christ can stand in His place. No mystical, fantasy Christ! No light within—as the spirit of Quakers extols—can diminish esteem of and dependence upon an outward Christ. The Spirit who gives testimony for this historical Jesus and leads to Him can be no other than the Spirit of God.

The devil has the most bitter and uncompromising hatred against Jesus, especially in His character as the Savior of men. The devil mortally hates the story and doctrine of Christ's redemption. Satan never would try to beget in men more honorable thoughts of Christ and lay greater weight on His instructions and commands. The Spirit who inclines men's hearts to the seed of the woman is not the spirit of the serpent that has such an irreconcilable hatred against Christ. He who heightens men's esteem of the glorious Michael, that prince of the angels, is not the spirit of the dragon who is at war with him.[3]

II. The Spirit Attacks Satan's Interests

When the Spirit who is at work operates against the interests of Satan's kingdom, this is a sure sign that He is a true and not a false spirit. Satan's kingdom lies in encouraging and establishing sin and cherishing men's worldly lusts. This sign we have given us in the fourth and fifth verses: "You, dear children, are from God and have overcome them, because the one who is in you is greater than the one who is in the world. They are from the world and therefore speak from the viewpoint of the world, and the world listens to them." Here is a plain antithesis. It is evident that the apostle is still comparing those who are influenced by two opposite kinds of spirits, the true and the false, and is showing the difference. The one is of God and overcomes the spirit of the world. The other is of the world and speaks and savors the things of the world. The spirit of the devil is here called "the one who is in the world." Christ says, "My kingdom is not of this world."[4] But it is otherwise with Satan's kingdom. He is "the god of this age."[5]

What the apostle means by the world or "the viewpoint of the world," we learn by his own words in the second chapter of this epistle, verses 15-16: "Do not love the world or anything in the world. If anyone loves the world, the love of the Father is not in him. For everything in the world—the cravings of sinful man, the lust of his eyes and the boasting of what he has and does—comes not from the Father but from the world." So by *the world* the apostle means everything that applies to the interest of sin. The term includes all the corruption and lusts of men and all the acts and objects by which they are gratified.

So we may safely determine, from what the apostle says, that there is a Spirit at work among people to lessen their esteem of the pleasures, profits, and honors of the world. This Spirit takes their hearts away from an eager pursuit after these things. He engages them in a deep concern about a future state and an eternal happiness that the Gospel reveals. He convinces them of the dreadfulness of sin. Considering the guilt he brings and the misery he exposes, he must be the Spirit of God.

It is not to be supposed that Satan would convince men of sin and awaken their consciences. It can no way serve his end to make that candle of the Lord shine brighter and to open the mouth of that governor of God in the soul. It is in his interest, whatever he does, to lull conscience to sleep and keep it quiet. To have conscience with its eyes and mouth open in the soul tends to hinder all Satan's designs of darkness and forever disturb his affairs. It thwarts the devil's interest and disturbs him so that he can manage nothing. Would the devil, when he is about to establish men in sin, first enlighten and awaken the conscience to see the dreadfulness of sin? Would the devil make them exceedingly afraid of sin and aware of their misery because of their past sins and their great need of deliverance from their guilt? Would he make them more careful, inquisitive, and watchful to discern what is sinful and to avoid future sins? Would he make them more afraid of his temptations and more careful to guard against them? What do those men do with their reason that suppose that the Spirit who operates thus is the spirit of the devil?

Some might say that the devil awakens men's consciences in order to deceive them. He makes them think they have been the subjects of a saving work of the Spirit of God though they are indeed still in the gall of bitterness. But to this it may be replied that the man who has an awakened conscience is the least likely to be deceived of all men in the world. It is the drowsy, unaware, stupid conscience that is most easily blinded. The more sensitive a conscience is in a diseased soul, the less easily it is quieted without a real healing. The more sensitive a conscience is to the dreadfulness of sin and the greatness of a man's own guilt, the less likely he is to rest in his own righteousness. The more sensitive a conscience is, the less likely it is to be pacified by shadows. A man who has been thoroughly terrified with a sense of his own danger and misery is not easily flattered and made to believe himself safe without any good grounds. To awaken conscience and convince it of the evil of sin cannot tend to establish sin but certainly tends to make way to cut out sin and Satan. Therefore this is a good argument that the Spirit who operates thus cannot be the spirit of the devil unless we suppose that Christ did not know how to argue. He told the Pharisees—who supposed that the spirit by which He worked was the spirit of the devil—that Satan would not cast out Satan.[6] Therefore, we may certainly conclude that the work is from the Spirit of God when the following conditions exist:

- Persons are sensitive to the dreadful nature of sin.
- People understand God's displeasure against sin.
- People are aware of their own miserable, sinful condition.
- They are earnestly concerned for their eternal salvation, and they are sensitive to their need of God's pity and help.

Such people seek salvation by using the means that God has appointed. When these conditions exist, we may be certain that the work is from the Spirit of God. There may be various effects of this work on their bodies. They may cry out aloud or shriek or faint. They may even go into convulsions, or the body and emotions may be moved in other ways.

> **The more sensitive a conscience is in a diseased soul, the less easily it is quieted without a real healing.**

The influence of the Spirit of God is even more clearly demonstrated when people have their hearts drawn away from the world. The Spirit weans them from the objects of their worldly lusts and takes from them worldly pursuits. He accomplishes this by giving them the sense of excellency of divine things and affection for spiritual enjoyments of another world that are promised in the Gospel.

III. *The Spirit Exalts the Holy Scriptures*

The Spirit who causes men to have greater regard for the Holy Scriptures and establishes them more in their truth and divine inspiration is certainly the Spirit of God. The apostle gives us this rule in the sixth verse. "We are from God, and whoever knows God listens to us; but whoever is not from God does not listen to us. This is how we recognize the Spirit of Truth and the spirit of falsehood." "*We are from God*"; that is, the apostles were sent by God and appointed by Him to teach the world and to deliver those doctrines and instructions that were to be our rule. "Whoever knows God listens to us."

The apostle's argument here equally teaches all who are of God—that is, all those God has appointed and inspired to deliver to His Church its rule of faith and practice. This refers to all the prophets and apostles whose doctrine God has made the foundation on which He has built His Church.[7] In a word, this means all the authors of the Holy Scriptures. The devil never would attempt to produce in persons a regard for that divine word. It is this very word that God has given to be the great and standing rule for the direction of His church in all spiritual matters and for all concerns of their souls in all ages. A spirit of delusion will not incline persons to seek direction from the mouth of God. "To the law and to the testimony!" is never the cry of evil spirits who have no light in them, for God directs us to discover their delusions. "When men tell you to consult mediums and spiritists, who whisper and mutter, should not a people inquire of their God? Why consult the dead on behalf of the living? To the law and to the testimony! If they do not speak according to this word, they have no light of dawn."[8] The devil does not say the same as Abraham did. "Abraham replied, 'They have Moses and the prophets; let them listen to them.'" Nor do they speak like the voice from heaven did concerning Christ: "This is my Son, whom I love. Listen to him!"[9]

Would the spirit of error, in order to deceive men, produce in them a high opinion of the infallible rule and incline them to think highly of it and be very familiar with it? Would the prince of darkness, to promote his kingdom of darkness, lead men to the sun? The devil has always shown a deadly spite and hatred toward that holy book, the Bible. He has done all in his power to extinguish that light and to draw men away from it. He knows it to be that light by which his kingdom of darkness will be overthrown. He has for many ages experienced its power to defeat his purposes and baffle his design. It is his constant plague. It is the main weapon that Michael uses in his war with him. It is the sword of the Spirit that pierces him and conquers him.[10] It is that great and strong sword with which God punishes Leviathan, that crooked serpent. It is that sharp sword that proceeds out of the mouth of him who sat on the horse, with which he smites his enemies.[11] Every text is a dart to torment the old serpent. He has felt the stinging smart thousands of times. Therefore, he is engaged against the Bible and hates every word in it. We may be sure that he never will attempt to raise persons' esteem of it or their affection for it. And accordingly, we see commonly in enthusiasts who oppose Christ that they depreciate this written rule and set up the light within their souls or some other rule above it.

IV. The Spirit Lifts Up Sound Doctrine

Another rule to judge the spirits may be drawn from those words used in addressing opposite spirits in the last words of the sixth verse: "The Spirit of truth and the spirit of falsehood." These words exhibit the two opposite characters of the Spirit of God and other spirits that counterfeit His operations. Therefore, if we observe that a spirit convinces people of those things that are true, we may safely determine that it is a right and true Spirit.[12] For instance, the true Spirit makes people more aware than they used to be that there is a God and that He is a great and a sin-hating God. The true Spirit impresses people that life is short and very uncertain and that there is another world. He shows them that they have immortal souls and must give account of themselves to God, they are exceedingly sinful by nature and practice, they are helpless in themselves. The true Spirit also confirms people in other things that are agreeable to sound doctrine. The Spirit who works thus operates as "the Spirit of truth." He represents things as they truly are. He brings men to the light, for whatever makes truth manifest is light. As the apostle Paul observes, "But everything exposed by the light becomes visible, for it is light that makes everything visible."[13] And therefore we may conclude that it is not the spirit of darkness who discovers and makes manifest the truth. Christ tells us that Satan is a liar and the father of lies.[14]

The devil's kingdom is a kingdom of darkness.[15] His kingdom is upheld and promoted only by darkness and error. Satan has all his power and dominion by darkness. Thus we read of the power of darkness.[16] And devils are called "the rulers of the darkness of this world."[17] Whatever spirit removes our darkness and brings us to the light undeceives us. The Spirit who convinces us of the truth does us a kindness. If I am brought to a sight of truth and am made aware of things as they really are, my duty is immediately to thank God for it without standing first to inquire by what means I have such a benefit.

V. The Spirit Promotes Love to God and Man

If the spirit who is at work among people operates as a spirit of love to God and man, it is a sure sign that it is the Spirit of God. This sign the apostle insists upon from the sixth verse to the end of the chapter. "We are from God, and whoever knows God listens to us; but whoever is not from God does not listen to us. This is how we recognize the Spirit of Truth and the spirit of falsehood. Dear friends, let us love one another, for love comes from God. Everyone who loves has been born of God and knows God. Whoever does not love does not know God, because God is love." Here the apostle is evidently still comparing those two sorts of persons who are influenced by the opposite kinds of spirits. He also mentions love as a mark by which we know who has the true Spirit. But this is especially evident by the twelfth and thirteenth verses: "If we love each other, God lives in us and his love is made complete in us. We know that we live in him and he in us, because he has given us of his Spirit." In these verses love is spoken of as if it were that of which the very nature of the Holy Spirit consists. It is as though divine love dwelling in us and the Spirit of God dwelling in us were the same thing. This is also seen in the last two verses of the previous chapter and in the sixteenth verse of this chapter.[18] Therefore, this last mark seems to be the most eminent, and thus the apostle insists much more largely upon it than upon all the rest. He speaks expressly of both love to God and men—of love to men in verses 7, 11, and 12,[19] of love to God in verses 17-19, of both in the last two verses, and of love to men as arising from love to God in those last two verses.[20]

Therefore, the Spirit working among the people brings many of them to high and exalting thoughts of the Divine Being and His glorious perfections. He develops in them an admiring, delightful sense of the excellency of Jesus Christ. He represents Christ as the chief among ten thousand and altogether lovely and makes Him precious to the soul. He wins and draws the heart with motives and encouragement to the love of which the apostle speaks in this passage of Scripture we are discussing. This is the wonderful, free love of God. He gave His one and only begotten Son to die for us when we were His enemies. This must be the work of the Spirit of God! As verses 9-10 say, "This is how God showed his love among us: He sent his one and only Son into the world that we might live through him. This is love: not that we loved God, but that he loved us and sent his Son as an atoning sacrifice for our sins." And verse 16 says, "And so we know and rely on the love God has for us. God is love. Whoever lives in love lives in God, and God in him." Verse 19 tells us, "We love because he first loved us." The Spirit excites love with these motives. He makes the attributes of God as revealed in the Gospel and manifested in Christ delightful objects of contemplation. He makes the soul long after God and Christ—after Their presence and communion, acquaintance with Them and conformity to Them; and to live to please and honor Them is the spirit that quells contentions among men. He gives a spirit of peace and goodwill. He excites acts of outward kindness and earnest desires for the salvation of souls. He causes a delight in those who appear as the children of God and followers of Christ. When a spirit operates after this manner among people, there is the highest kind of evidence of the influence of a true and divine Spirit.

Indeed, there is a counterfeit love that often appears among those who are led by a spirit of delusion. There is usually in the wildest enthusiasm a kind of union and affection. This arises from self-love caused by men agreeing in those things in which they greatly differ from all others. These differences make them objects of the ridicule of all the rest of mankind. This ridicule naturally will cause them so much the more to prize those peculiarities that make them the objects of others' contempt. Thus the ancient Gnostics and the wild fanatics who appeared at the beginning of the Reformation boasted of their great love one to another. One sect of them in particular called themselves "the family of love." But this is quite another thing than that Christian love I have just described. It is only the working of a natural self-love. It is not true benevolence any more than the union and friendship that may be seen among a company of pirates who are at war with all the rest of the world. There is enough said in this passage of the nature of a truly Christian love to thoroughly distinguish it from all such counterfeits. It is love that arises from grasping with the mind the wonderful riches of the free grace and sovereignty of God's love to us in Jesus Christ. It is sensing our own utter unworthiness. It is recognizing ourselves to be the enemies and haters of God and Christ. It requires a renunciation of all our own excellency and righteousness.[21]

What is the surest character of true, divine, supernatural love that distinguishes it from counterfeits that arise from a natural self-love? It is the Christian virtue of humility that shines in it. Divine love above all others renounces and abases what we term "self." Christian love or true love is a humble love. "Love is patient, love is kind. It does not envy, it does not boast, it is not proud. It is not rude, it is not self-seeking, it is not easily angered, it keeps no record of wrongs."[22]

What are the characteristics of a person who dwells in love, who dwells in God and God in him? In that person we see a sense of his own smallness, vileness, weakness, and utter insufficiency. We see a lack of self-confidence. We see self-emptiness, self-denial, and poverty of spirit. These are the manifest tokens of the Spirit of God. What the apostle speaks of as a great evidence of the true Spirit is God's love or Christ's love. "His love is made complete in us."[23] We may see best what kind of love this is in what appeared in Christ's example. The love that appeared in the Lamb of God was not only a love to friends but to enemies.[24] It was love with a meek and humble spirit. "Learn from me," says He, "for I am gentle and humble in heart."[25] Love and humility are the two things more contrary to the devil than anything in the world. The character of the devil, above all things, consists of pride and malice.

> **Love and humility are the two things more contrary to the devil than anything in the world. The character of the devil, above all things, consists of pride and malice.**

Thus, I have spoken especially of the particular marks the apostle gives us of a work of the true Spirit. Some of these things the devil would not do if he could. He would not awaken the conscience and make men aware of their miserable state caused by sin. He would not make them aware of their great need of a Savior. The devil would not confirm men in the belief that Jesus is the Son of God and the Savior of sinners or raise men's value and esteem of Him. He would not generate in men's minds an opinion of the necessity, usefulness, and truth of the Holy Scriptures or induce them to make much use of them. Nor would he show men the truth in things that concern their souls' interest. He would not undeceive them and lead them out of darkness into light. He would not give them a view of things as they really are.

And here are other things the devil neither can nor will do. He will not give men a spirit of divine love or Christian humility and poverty of spirit, nor could he if he wanted to. He cannot give things he has not himself. Divine love, Christian humility, and poverty of spirit are as contrary as possible to his nature. Therefore, when there is an extraordinary influence or operation appearing on the minds of people, if these things are found in it, we are safe in determining that it is the work of God. Many other circumstances may accompany it. Many other instruments may be used. Many other methods may be used to promote it. God is sovereign. His judgments are a great deep. He carries them out no matter what may be the motion of the sensual spirits. He carries them out no matter what may be the effects wrought on men's bodies. These marks that the apostle has given us are sufficient to stand alone and support themselves. They plainly show the finger of God[26] and are sufficient to outweigh a thousand such little objections as many make from oddities, irregularities, errors in conduct, and the delusions and scandals of some who profess to know God. But here some may object to the sufficiency of the marks in light of what the apostle Paul says: "For such men are false apostles, deceitful workmen, masquerading as apostles of Christ. And no wonder, for Satan himself masquerades as an angel of light."[27]

It can be no objection against the sufficiency of these marks to distinguish the true from the false spirit in those false apostles and prophets. The devil was transformed into an angel of light. It is principally with a view to them that the apostle gives these marks. Notice the words of the text: "Do not believe every spirit, but test the spirits to see whether they are from God,"[28] and this is the reason he gives: "Because many false prophets have gone out into the world." It is as though the apostle John says, "There are many gone out into the world who are the ministers of the devil and who transform themselves into prophets of God in whom the spirit of the devil is transformed into an angel of light. Therefore, try the spirits by these rules that I will give you. Then you will be able to distinguish the true spirit from the false who use such a crafty disguise."

Those false prophets the apostle John speaks of are doubtless the same sort of men as those "false apostles" and "deceitful workmen" the apostle Paul speaks of. In these people the devil was transformed into an angel of light. Therefore, we may be sure that these marks are especially adapted to distinguish between the true Spirit and the devil transformed into an angel of light. The distinguishing marks are given especially for that end. That is the apostle's declared purpose and design, to give marks by which the true Spirit may be distinguished from that sort of counterfeit.

Look over what is said about those false prophets and false apostles (there is much said about them in the New Testament). Take notice in what manner the devil was transformed into an angel of light in them. Then we shall not find anything that in the least injures the sufficiency of these marks to distinguish the true Spirit from such counterfeits. The devil transformed himself into an angel of light, for there was in the "false apostles" and "deceitful workmen" a show and great boast of extraordinary knowledge in divine things.[29] Hence their followers called themselves Gnostics, from their great, pretended knowledge. And the devil in them mimicked the miraculous gifts of the Holy Spirit in visions, revelations, prophecies, miracles, etc. Hence they are called false apostles and false prophets.[30]

Again, there was a false show of and lying pretensions to great holiness and devotion in words.[31] Hence they are called deceitful workers and wells and clouds without water.[32] There was also in them a show of extraordinary piety and righteousness in their superstitious worship.[33] So they had a false, proud, and bitter zeal.[34] They also exhibited a false show of humility in affecting an extraordinary outward baseness and dejection when indeed their "unspiritual minds" puffed them up with "idle notions" and made a righteousness of their humility so that they were proud of their public piety.[35] But how do such things as these in the least injure those things that have been mentioned as the distinguishing evidences of the true Spirit? In addition to such vain shows that may be from the devil, there are common influences of the Spirit that are often mistaken for saving grace; but though they are not saving, they are the work of the true Spirit.

Having thus fulfilled what I first proposed in considering what are the certain, distinguishing marks by which we may safely proceed in judging any work that falls under our observation, whether it be the work of the Spirit of God or no, I now proceed to the *application*.

FOOTNOTES TO THIS SECTION

1. Matthew 10:32; Romans 15:9; Philippians 2:11.

2. 1 Corinthians 12:3.

3. "But the prince of the Persian kingdom resisted me twenty-one days. Then Michael, one of the chief princes, came to help me, because I was detained there with the king of Persia . . . but first I will tell you what is written in the Book of Truth. (No one supports me against them except Michael, your prince.) . . . At that time Michael, the great prince who protects your people, will arise. There will be a time of distress such as has not happened from the beginning of nations until then. But at that time your people— everyone whose name is found written in the book—will be delivered" (Daniel 10:13, 21; 12:1).

4. John 18:36.

5. 2 Corinthians 4:4.

6. "Jesus knew their thoughts and said to them, 'Every kingdom divided against itself will be ruined, and every city or household divided against itself will not stand. If Satan drives out Satan, he is divided against himself. How then can his kingdom stand?'" (Matthew 12:25-26).

7. "Built on the foundation of the apostles and prophets, with Christ Jesus himself as the chief cornerstone" (Ephesians 2:20).

8. Isaiah 8:19-20.

9. Luke 16:29; Mark 9:7.

10. Hebrews 4:12.

11. "Out of his mouth comes a sharp sword with which to strike down the nations. 'He will rule them with an iron scepter.' He treads the winepress of the fury of the wrath of God Almighty" (Revelation 19:15).

12. "When he comes, he will convict the world of guilt in regard to sin and righteousness and judgment: in regard to sin, because men do not believe in me; in regard to righteousness, because I am going to the Father, where you can see me no longer; and in regard to judgment, because the prince of this world now stands condemned" (John 16:8).

13. Ephesians 5:13-14.

14. "You belong to your father, the devil, and you want to carry out your father's desire. He was a murderer from the beginning, not holding to the truth, for there is no truth in him. When he lies, he speaks his native language, for he is a liar and the father of lies" (John 8:44).

15. "To open their eyes and turn them from darkness to light, and from the power of Satan to God, so that they may receive forgiveness of sins and a place among those who are sanctified by faith in me" (Acts 26:18).

16. "Every day I was with you in the temple courts, and you did not lay a hand on me. But this is your hour—when darkness reigns" (Luke 22:53). "For he has rescued us from the dominion of darkness and brought us into the kingdom of the Son he loves" (Colossians 1:13).

17. *King James Version*; NIV: "For our struggle is not against flesh and blood, but against the rulers, against the authorities, against the powers of this dark world and against the spiritual forces of evil in the heavenly realms" (Ephesians 6:12).

18. "And this is his command: to believe in the name of his Son, Jesus Christ, and to love one another as he commanded us. Those who obey his commands live in him, and he in them. And this is how we know that he lives in us: We know it by the Spirit he gave us" (1 John 3:23-24). "And so we know and rely on the love God has for us. God is love. Whoever lives in love lives in God, and God in him" (1 John 4:16).

19. "Dear friends, let us love one another, for love comes from God. Everyone who loves has been born of God and knows God. . . . Dear friends, since God so loved us, we also ought to love one another. No one has ever seen God; but if we love each other, God lives in us and his love is made complete in us" (1 John 4:7, 11-12).

20. "If anyone says, 'I love God,' yet hates his brother, he is a liar. For anyone

who does not love his brother, whom he has seen, cannot love God, whom he has not seen. And he has given us this command: Whoever loves God must also love his brother" (1 John 4:20-21).

21. "This is how God showed his love among us: He sent his one and only Son into the world that we might live through him. This is love: not that we loved God, but that he loved us and sent his Son as an atoning sacrifice for our sins. Dear friends, since God so loved us, we also ought to love one another. . . . We love because he first loved us" (1 John 4:9-11, 19)

22. 1 Corinthians 13:4-5.

23. 1 John 4:12.

24. "But I tell you: Love your enemies and pray for those who persecute you" (Matthew 5:44) "Jesus said, 'Father, forgive them, for they do not know what they are doing.' And they divided up his clothes by casting lots" (Luke 23:34).

25. Matthew 11:29-30.

26. "Then the LORD said to Moses, 'Tell Aaron, "Stretch out your staff and strike the dust of the ground," and throughout the land of Egypt the dust will become gnats.' They did this, and when Aaron stretched out his hand with the staff and struck the dust of the ground, gnats came upon men and animals. All the dust throughout the land of Egypt became gnats. But when the magicians tried to produce gnats by their secret arts, they could not. And the gnats were on men and animals. The magicians said to Pharaoh, 'This is the finger of God.' But Pharaoh's heart was hard and he would not listen, just as the LORD had said" (Exodus 8:16-19). "Jesus was driving out a demon that was mute. When the demon left, the man who had been mute spoke, and the crowd was amazed. But some of them said, 'By Beelzebub, the prince of demons, he is driving out demons.' Others tested him by asking for a sign from heaven. Jesus knew their thoughts and said to them: 'Any kingdom divided against itself will be ruined, and a house divided against itself will fall. If Satan is divided against himself, how can his kingdom stand? I say this because you claim that I drive out demons by Beelzebub. Now if I drive out demons by Beelzebub, by whom do your followers drive them out? So then, they will be your judges. But if I drive out demons by the finger of God, then the kingdom of God has come to you'" (Luke 11:14-20).

27. 2 Corinthians 11:13-14.

28. 1 John 4:1.

29. "See to it that no one takes you captive through hollow and deceptive philosophy, which depends on human tradition and the basic principles of this world rather than on Christ" (Colossians 2:8). "Some have wandered away from these and turned to meaningless talk. They want to be teachers of the law, but they do not know what they are talking about or what they so confidently affirm" (1 Timothy 1:6-7). "If anyone teaches false doctrines and does not agree to the sound instruction of our Lord Jesus Christ and to godly teaching, he is conceited and understands nothing. He has an unhealthy interest in controversies and quarrels about words that result in

envy, quarreling, malicious talk, evil suspicions and constant friction between men of corrupt mind, who have been robbed of the truth and who think that godliness is a means to financial gain" (1 Timothy 6:3-5). "Keep reminding them of these things. Warn them before God against quarreling about words; it is of no value and only ruins those who listen. Do your best to present yourself to God as one approved, a workman who does not need to be ashamed and who correctly handles the word of truth. Avoid godless chatter, because those who indulge in it will become more and more ungodly. Their teaching will spread like gangrene. Among them are Hymenaeus and Philetus, who have wandered away from the truth. They say that the resurrection has already taken place, and they destroy the faith of some" (2 Timothy 2:14-18). "For there are many rebellious people, mere talkers and deceivers, especially those of the circumcision group" (Titus 1:10). "They claim to know God, but by their actions they deny him. They are detestable, disobedient and unfit for doing anything good" (Titus 1:16).

30. "For false Christs and false prophets will appear and perform great signs and miracles to deceive even the elect—if that were possible" (Matthew 24:24).

31. "I urge you, brothers, to watch out for those who cause divisions and put obstacles in your way that are contrary to the teaching you have learned. Keep away from them. For such people are not serving our Lord Christ, but their own appetites. By smooth talk and flattery they deceive the minds of naive people" (Romans 16:17-18). "Then we will no longer be infants, tossed back and forth by the waves, and blown here and there by every wind of teaching and by the cunning and craftiness of men in their deceitful scheming" (Ephesians 4:14).

32. "For such men are false apostles, deceitful workmen, masquerading as apostles of Christ" (2 Corinthians 11:13). "These men are springs without water and mists driven by a storm. Blackest darkness is reserved for them" (2 Peter 2:17). "These men are blemishes at your love feasts, eating with you without the slightest qualm—shepherds who feed only themselves. They are clouds without rain, blown along by the wind; autumn trees without fruit and uprooted—twice dead" (Jude 12).

33. "Therefore do not let anyone judge you by what you eat or drink, or with regard to a religious festival, a New Moon celebration or a Sabbath day. These are a shadow of the things that were to come; the reality, however, is found in Christ. Do not let anyone who delights in false humility and the worship of angels disqualify you for the prize. Such a person goes into great detail about what he has seen, and his unspiritual mind puffs him up with idle notions. He has lost connection with the Head, from whom the whole body, supported and held together by its ligaments and sinews, grows as God causes it to grow. Since you died with Christ to the basic principles of this world, why, as though you still belonged to it, do you submit to its rules: 'Do not handle! Do not taste! Do not touch!'? These are all destined to perish with use, because they are based on human commands and teachings. Such regulations indeed have an appearance of wisdom, with their self-imposed worship, their false humility and their harsh treatment of the

body, but they lack any value in restraining sensual indulgence" (Colossians 2:16-22).

34. "Those people are zealous to win you over, but for no good. What they want is to alienate you [from us], so that you may be zealous for them. It is fine to be zealous, provided the purpose is good, and to be so always and not just when I am with you" (Galatians 4:17). "Some have wandered away from these and turned to meaningless talk" (1 Timothy 1:6). "He is conceited and understands nothing. He has an unhealthy interest in controversies and arguments that result in envy, quarreling, malicious talk, evil suspicions and constant friction between men of corrupt mind, who have been robbed of the truth and who think that godliness is a means to financial gain" (1 Timothy 6:4).

35. "Do not let anyone who delights in false humility and the worship of angels disqualify you for the prize. Such a person goes into great detail about what he has seen, and his unspiritual mind puffs him up with idle notions. . . . Such regulations indeed have an appearance of wisdom, with their self-imposed worship, their false humility and their harsh treatment of the body, but they lack any value in restraining sensual indulgence" (Colossians 2:18, 23).

PRACTICAL INFERENCES

I. The Recent Extraordinary Influence Is from the Spirit of God

From what has been said, I will venture to draw this inference: The recent extraordinary influence causing rare concern and engagement of mind about the Christian faith is undoubtedly, in general, from the Spirit of God. Only two things are needed to judge a work—rules and facts. The rules of the word of God we have had laid before us. And as to facts, there are but two ways to compare them with the rules. Either we judge by our own observation or by information from others who have had opportunity to observe them.

There are many things concerning this work that are well known. These are sufficient to determine it to be the work of God, unless the apostle John was incorrect in his rules. The Spirit who is at work takes people's minds off the vanities of the world. He engages them in a deep concern about eternal happiness. He puts their thoughts on earnestly seeking their salvation. He convinces them of the dreadfulness of sin and of their own guile and miserable natural state. The Spirit awakens men's consciences and makes them aware of God's awful anger. He causes in them a great desire and earnest care and endeavor to obtain God's favor. He causes them to be more diligent in the use of His appointed means of grace. Especially, this is seen in a greater desire to hear and read the word of God. And it is well known that the Spirit who is at work operates as the Spirit of truth. He makes people more aware of what is really true in those things that concern their eternal salvation. He impresses on them that they must die and that life is very short and uncertain. He shows them there is a great sin-hating God to whom they are accountable and who will fix them in an eternal state in another world. He shows them they stand in great need of a Savior. He makes persons more aware of the value of Jesus who was crucified and their need of Him. And this awareness moves them earnestly to seek an interest in Him.

These things should be apparent to people throughout the land, for these things are not done in a corner. The work has not been confined to a few towns in some more remote parts. The work has been carried on in many places all over the land and in most of the principal, populous, and public places in it. Christ, in this respect, has worked among us in the same manner that He did His miracles in Judea. This has now been continued for a long time, so that there has been a great opportunity to observe the manner of the work. And all who have been very familiar with the people involved in this work see even more that, by the rules of the apostle, this is clearly and certainly the work of God.

How can the nature and tendency of a spirit that is at work be determined with certainty and less danger of being misunderstood? This can be determined when we see it in a great many people of all sorts and in various places. Broad observation gives more credibility than when the work of the Spirit is only seen in a few that have been very familiar one with another in some particular place. A few specific people may agree to defraud others. They may profess things that they never experienced. But this is difficult to do when the work is spread over many parts of a country, in places distant from one another, among people of all sorts and of all ages and in multitudes possessed of a sound mind, good understanding, and known integrity.

It would be absolute absurdity to suppose from all the evidence that it cannot yet be determined what kind of influence they are under. Can it not be determined whether it tends to awaken their consciences or to stupefy them? Does it incline them more to seek their salvation or neglect it? Does it seem to confirm them in a belief of the Scriptures or to lead them to deism?[1] Does it make them have more regard for the great truths of the Christian faith or less?

Some people profess that they are convinced of certain divine truths to the point that they esteem and love them in a saving manner. Others profess that they are only more convinced or confirmed in the truth of them than they used to be. These are two very different things. Honest persons with common sense have much greater right to demand that credit be given to being confirmed in the truth than to loving divine truth in a saving manner. Indeed, in loving divine truth in a saving manner, it is less likely that large groups of people should be deceived than some isolated individuals. Are convictions and the change in dispositions and emotions saving? This question is beyond the present scope of discussion; however, these effects on people are signs of the influence of the Spirit of God—whether or not they are saving. Scripture's rules distinguish common influences of the Spirit of God and those that are saving.

By the providence of God I have for some months been much

among those who have experienced the work in question. Particularly, I have been observing those extraordinary things with which many persons have been offended—such as people crying out aloud, shrieking, and being put into great agonies of body. I have seen the manner and results of such operations and the fruits of them. I have been closely associated with many of the persons before and since their souls' concerns. So I consider myself called now to give my testimony that this work has all those marks that have been pointed out. This has been the case in very many instances, and all those marks have appeared in a very great degree.

The people experiencing these uncommon appearances have been of two sorts. Some have been in great distress from a foreboding of their sin and misery. Others have been overcome with a sweet sense of the greatness, wonderfulness, and excellency of divine things. I have observed multitudes concerned about their sin. Very few had their distress from improper conviction. Most were very aware of the truth. People were under intense restraints to avoid outward show of their distress, but I do not think they would have done otherwise. Very few appeared to feign or affect such public demonstrations. Very many could absolutely not have avoided it. Generally, in these agonies they have appeared to be in the perfect exercise of their reason. Those of them who could speak have been well able to give an account of the circumstances of their mind and the cause of their distress at the time. And they were able to remember and give an account of it afterwards. I have known very few people who, in their great excess, have briefly been deprived in some measure of reason. And among the many hundreds—maybe thousands—who have recently experienced such distresses, I have never yet known one permanently deprived of reason. Some I have known were visibly sad. Their distresses are of another kind and operate quite after another manner than when their distress is from mere conviction.

It is not truth only that distresses them but many vain shadows and notions that will not give place either to Scripture or reason. Some in their great distress have not been well able to give an account of themselves or to declare the understanding they have of things. They have not been able to explain the manner and cause of their trouble to others; yet I have had no reason to think they were not under proper convictions. But those who have had much to do with souls under spiritual difficulties will not at all question this. Some things are new to them, such as their ideas and inward sensations. This is, therefore, impossible to express in words. Some, on first investigation, said they knew not what was the matter with them. However, when they were individually examined, they were able to explain their case, though without help they could not.

Some suppose that terrors producing such effects are only mere fright. But certainly there ought to be a distinction made between intense but fully proportional distress caused by fear of a terrifying truth and the effects produced by a needless and causeless fright. The causeless fright is of two kinds. Either persons are terrified with that which is not the truth (of which I have seen very few instances unless in cases of depression); or they are frightened from some terrible outward appearance and noise and a general notion arising from it. These fear that there is at hand something terrible—they know not what. They have in their minds no particular truth whatever. Of such a kind of fear I have seen very little among either old or young.

Those who are in such extremes usually express a great sense of their excessive wickedness and the many aggravations of their actual sins. They realize their dreadful pollution, hostility, and rottenness. They acknowledge their obstinacy and hardness of heart. They sense their great guilt in the sight of God, and they know the dreadfulness of the punishment due to sin. Very often they have a vivid idea of the horrible pit of eternal misery. At the same time, it appears that the great God who has them in His hands is exceedingly angry—His wrath appears amazingly terrible to them. God appears to them much provoked and His great wrath increased. They are apprehensive of great danger, sensing that He will not bear with them any longer. Now they fear He will immediately cut them off and send them down to the dreadful pit they have in view. At the same time, they see no refuge. They see more and more of the vanity of everything they used to trust and with which they flattered themselves. They are brought to total despair, and they see that they are at the disposal of the will of that God who is so angry with them. Very many, in the midst of their extremity, have been brought to an extraordinary sense of their fully deserving that wrath and the destruction that was then before their eyes. They fear every moment that it will be executed upon them. They have been greatly convinced that this would be altogether just and that God is indeed absolutely sovereign.

Very often some text of Scripture expressing God's sovereignty has been impressed upon their minds. By this they have been calmed. They have been brought, as it were, to lie at God's feet. And after great agonies they have been composed and quiet in submission to a just and sovereign God. Their bodily strength was exhausted. It appeared their lives were almost gone. Then light appeared. A glorious Redeemer and His wonderful, all-sufficient grace was pictured in some sweet invitation of Scripture. Sometimes the light came in suddenly. Sometimes the light came more gradually, filling their souls with love, admiration, joy, and self-abasement. Their hearts were drawn after the excellent lovely Redeemer. They longed to lie in the dust before Him. And they longed that others might behold, embrace, and be delivered by Him. They had longings to live to His glory but were aware that they could do nothing of themselves. They appeared vile in their own eyes. They had much jealousy over their own hearts. All the appearances of a real change of heart had followed. Grace acted as it used to act in those who were converted. This grace acted with similar difficulties, temptations, batterings, and comforts. But in many, the light and comfort had been in higher degrees than ordinary.

Many very young children have been thus acted upon. There have been some instances very much like those of which we read in Mark's Gospel: "The evil spirit shook the man violently and came out of him with a shriek."[2] Probably those instances were designed to be a type of such things as these. Some people have several cycles of great agonies before they are delivered. And others have been in distress that passed, though no deliverance followed.

Some object to emotional displays as being great confusion when there is a number together in such circumstances making a noise. They say that God cannot be the author of it. He is the

God of order, not of confusion. Such confusion breaks the order of things. Order is achieved when things are properly disposed and duly directed to their end. When the order and due connection of means is broken, they fail in their end. Now the conviction of sinners for their conversion is the obtaining of the end of religious means. But I do not think the people so extraordinarily moved should try to refrain from such outward expressions. They can and should refrain to their utmost at the time of their solemn worship. But God may so convince people's consciences that they must express it outwardly. They may even interrupt and break off the public services they attend. This is not confusion or an unhappy interruption. A group of people may meet on the field to pray for rain and stop praying because there is a torrential downpour of rain. Oh, that all the public assemblies in the land were interrupted with such confusion on this next Sabbath day! We need not be sorry for breaking the order of service by obtaining an end to which that order is directed. He who is going to fetch a treasure need not be sorry that meeting the treasure in the midst of his journey stops him.

Besides those who are overcome with conviction and distress, I have recently seen many who have had their bodily strength taken away. This weakness is caused by a sense of the glorious excellency of the Redeemer and the wonders of His dying love. They also have a very uncommon sense of their own smallness and great sordidness. And they express and show the greatest humbling and loathing of themselves. New converts and many who were formerly converted have had their love and joy joined with a flood of tears. The formerly converted have shown contrition and humiliation, especially for their having not lived more to God's glory since their conversion. These have had a far greater sight of their vileness and the evil of their hearts than they ever had. Also, they have a passionate desire to live better in the future and to be attended by greater self-denial than ever. Many have been overcome with pity for the souls of others and longing for their salvation. I might mention many other things in this extraordinary work, each of which would be verified by all of those marks on which we have insisted. The apostle John would approve this as a work of the true Spirit.

Providence has put me in a place where the work of God has been carried on with careful attention to form and detail. I had the happiness to be seated in that place two years with the venerable Stoddard. And I then knew a number of people who during that season were deeply moved under his ministry. I have been closely associated with the experiences of many others who were deeply moved under his ministry before that period, in a manner agreeable to the doctrine of all orthodox divines. And lately a work has been carried on there with many unusual actions. But it is, to all outward appearances, the same work that was carried on there in different periods, though with some new circumstances. And certainly if this is not the work of God, we must discard all talk of conversion and Christian experience. We must throw away our Bibles and give up revealed Christian faith. Not that I suppose the degree of the Spirit's influence is to be determined by the degree of effect on men's bodies. Nor do I suppose that the best experiences are always those that have the greatest influence on the body.

And now let us consider the rash acts, irregularities, and mixture of delusion that have been observed. Reformation comes after a long continued and almost universal deadness. We should not wonder that when the revival is new, it is attended with such things. In the first creation God did not make a complete world at once. There was a great deal of imperfection before the whole stood in perfect form. There was darkness and a mixture of chaos and confusion even after God first said, "Let there be light."[3] God at first began His great work to deliver His people after their long continued bondage in Egypt. When He did this, there were false wonders mixed with the true for a while. These false wonders hardened the unbelieving Egyptians and made them doubt the divine origin of the whole work. When the children of Israel first went to bring up the ark of God, it had been neglected and long absent. But they did not seek the Lord in the proper manner.[4] At the time when the sons of God came to present themselves before the Lord, Satan also came among them.[5] And Solomon's ships, when they brought gold, silver, and pearls, also brought apes and baboons.[6]

When daylight first appears after a night of darkness, we must expect to have darkness mixed with light for a while. We will not have perfect day and the sun risen all at once. The fruits of the earth are first green before they are ripe, and they come to their proper perfection gradually. So, Christ tells us, is the kingdom of God. "This is what the kingdom of God is like. A man scatters seed on the ground. Night and day, whether he sleeps or gets up, the seed sprouts and grows, though he does not know how. All by itself the soil produces grain—first the stalk, then the head, then the full kernel in the head."[7]

Mainly young persons have been the subjects of this work. They have less stability and experience. In the heat of youth they are much more ready to run to extremes. Thus their reckless acts and errors are the less to be wondered at. Satan will keep his grip on men as long as he can. But when he can do that no longer, he often tries to drive them to extremes. Satan wants them to dishonor God and wound the Christian faith in that way. There have been occasions of much misconduct. And many people see plainly that their ministers have an ill opinion of the work. Therefore, with just reason their ministers dare not apply themselves as their people's guides; and so we are without guides.

It is no wonder then that people, like sheep without a shepherd, wander out of the way. People in such circumstances stand in great and continual need of guides, and their guides stand in continual need of much more wisdom than their own. People may have ministers who favor the work and rejoice in it. Yet we should not expect that either the people or ministers should know well how to conduct themselves in such an extraordinary state of things. The situation is new, and they never had any experience of it before. They did not have time to see the work's trends, results, and effects. The happy influence of experience is very manifest today in the people among whom God has established His home. The work carried on there this year is much purer than that which was wrought there six years before. It seems to be more purely spiritual. It is free from natural and corrupt mixtures. It has nothing savoring of enthusiastic wildness and extravagance. It works more by deep humiliation and abasement before God and men. They have been much freer from foolhardy acts and irregularities. There has been a remarkable difference in this respect. Before, in their comforts and rejoicings, they did too much forget their distance from God. They were ready in their discussion of the things of God and of their own experiences to talk with too much levity. But now they seem to have no tendency that way. They rejoice with a more solemn, reverential, humble joy, as God directs.[8] The joy is as great and in many instances much greater. Many among us upon whom He worked in that former season have now had much greater communications from heaven than they had then. Their rejoicing operates in another manner. It abases them, breaks their hearts, and brings them into the dust. When they speak of their joys, it is not with laughter but a flood of tears. Thus those who laughed before weep now. Yet by their united testimony their joy is vastly purer and sweeter than that which before did raise their sensual spirits. They are now more like Jacob when God appeared to him at Bethel. When he saw the ladder that reached to heaven, he said, "How awesome is this place!"[9] And they are like Moses when God showed him His glory on the mount, when he made haste and "bowed to the ground at once and worshiped."[10]

II. We Should Do Our Utmost to Promote It

For the reasons we have considered, let us all be warned. We should not oppose or do anything in the least to clog or hinder the work. On the contrary, we should do our utmost to promote it. Now Christ is come down from heaven in a remarkable and wonderful work of His Spirit. It is proper for all His professed disciples to acknowledge Him and give Him honor.

The example of the Jews in Christ's and the apostles' times should teach those who do not acknowledge this work to be very cautious of what they say or do. Christ then was in the world, and the world knew Him not: He came to His own professing people, and His own received Him not.[11] That coming of Christ was much spoken of in the biblical prophecies that they had in their hands. It had been long expected. Yet because Christ came in a manner they did not expect and that did not conform to their human reason, they would not own Him. Rather, they opposed Him, counted Him a madman, and pronounced the Spirit by which He worked to be the spirit of the devil. They stood and wondered at the great things done. They knew not what to make of them. Yet they erected so many stumbling blocks that they finally could not acknowledge Him. And when the Spirit of God was poured out so wonderfully in the apostles' days, they looked upon it as confusion and distraction. They were astonished by what they saw and heard but were not convinced. The work of God was rejected, especially by those who were most conceited about their own understanding and knowledge. As Scripture says, "Therefore once more I will astound these people with wonder upon wonder; the wisdom of the wise will perish, the intelligence of the intelligent will vanish."[12] And many with a reputation for religion and piety had great spite against the work. They saw that the work tended to diminish their honor and to express disapproval of their formality and lukewarmness. Some, upon these accounts, maliciously and openly opposed and reproached the work of the Spirit of God. They called it the work of the devil, against inward conviction. Thus they were guilty of the unpardonable sin against the Holy Spirit.

There is another spiritual coming of Christ to set up His kingdom in the world. That spiritual coming of Christ is as much spoken of in Scripture prophecy as the first coming. It has long been expected by the Church of God. We have reason to think from what is said of this that it will be in many respects parallel with the other. And certainly that low state into which the visible church of God has lately been sunk is very parallel with the state of the Jewish church when Christ came. Therefore, it is no wonder at all that when Christ comes, His work should appear a strange work to most. Yes, it would be a wonder if it should be otherwise. The present work may not be the beginning of that great and frequently predicted coming of Christ to set up His kingdom. But it is evident from what has been said that it is a work of the same Spirit and of the same nature. There is no reason to doubt that persons who persistently refuse to acknowledge Christ in the work will provoke God. This is how it was with the Jews of old. They refused to acknowledge Christ. They may plead that great stumbling blocks are in the way and therefore they have to doubt the work. The teachers of the Jewish church found countless obstacles that were to them impossible to overcome. Many things appeared in Christ and in the work of the Spirit after His ascension that were very strange to them. They were certain they had just cause for their scruples. Christ and His work were to the Jews a stumbling block.[13] "Blessed is the man," said Christ, "who does not fall away on account of me."[14] The manner of Christ's appearance was strange and unexpected. He had not been in Judea working miracles long before all those who observed and yet refused to acknowledge Him brought fearful guilt upon themselves in the sight of God. And Christ condemned those who could discern the face of the sky and of the earth, yet could not discern the signs of those times. "Why," said He, "don't you judge for yourselves what is right?"[15]

The great Jehovah placed the rainbow in the heavens. Now He has appeared here for a certain length of time, in such a glorious work of His power and grace. This He did in an extensive manner, in the most public places of the land, and in almost all parts of it. He has given such evidences of His presence that great numbers, and even many teachers in His Church, cannot remain guiltless in His sight. They must receive and acknowledge Him. They should give Him honor and rejoice in His gracious presence. But instead they do not so much as once give Him thanks for so glorious and blessed a work of His grace. In this work of grace, His goodness is seen more than if He had bestowed on us all the temporal blessings that the world affords. A long-continued silence in the light of this gracious work is undoubtedly provoking to God, especially in ministers. It is a secret kind of opposition that really tends to hinder the work. Such silent ministers stand in the way of the work of God. As Christ said of old, "He who is not with me is against me."[16]

Some stand wondering at this strange work. They do not know what to make of it. They refuse to receive it. Sometimes they speak contemptibly of it. This was the case with the Jews of old. They would do well to consider and to tremble at St. Paul's words to them: "Take care that what the prophets have said does not happen to you: 'Look, you scoffers, wonder and perish, for I am going to do something in your days that you would never believe, even if someone told you.'"[17] Those who cannot believe the work to be true because of the extraordinary degree and manner of it should consider how it was with the unbelieving officer in Samaria. He said, "Look, even if the LORD should open the floodgates of the heavens, could this happen?" In reply

Elisha said, "You will see it with your own eyes, but you will not eat any of it!"[18] To the Egyptians the pillar of cloud and fire was darkness, though it gave light to God's Israel. Let all to whom this work is a cloud and darkness take heed that it not be their destruction!

Some convince themselves that they are acting prudently by waiting to see the results of things. They wait to see what fruits those who are the subjects of this work will bring forth in their lives and conduct. I plead with them to consider whether this justifies a long refraining from acknowledging Christ when He appears so wonderfully and graciously present in the land. It is probable that many of those who are thus waiting know not for what they are waiting. If they wait to see a work of God without difficulties and stumbling blocks, it will be like a fool waiting at the riverside to have the water all run by. A work of God without stumbling blocks is never to be expected. "Such things must come."[19] There never yet was any great manifestation that God made of Himself to the world without many difficulties attending it. The works of God, like His Word, seem at first full of things that are strange, inconsistent, and difficult to the carnal, unbelieving hearts of men. Christ and His work always were, and always will be, a stone of stumbling, a rock of offense, a snare to many.[20] The prophet Hosea speaks of a glorious revival of religion in God's church. God will be as the dew unto Israel. Israel will grow as the lily and cast forth her roots as Lebanon, whose branches should spread. Hosea concludes, "Who is wise? He will realize these things. Who is discerning? He will understand them. The ways of the LORD are right; the righteous walk in them, but the rebellious stumble in them."[21]

If they wait to see a work of God without difficulties and stumbling blocks, it will be like a fool waiting at the riverside to have the water all run by. A work of God without stumbling blocks is never to be expected.

It is probable that the stumbling blocks that now attend this work will in some respects be increased and not diminished. We probably shall see more instances of apostasy and gross iniquity among those who profess faith. And if one kind of stumbling block is removed, it is to be expected that others will come. It is with Christ's works as it was with His parables. Things that are difficult to men's dark minds are ordered on purpose for the trial of their disposition and spiritual sense. And those of corrupt minds and of an unbelieving, perverse, petty, fault-finding spirit are described thus: "though seeing, they may not see; though hearing, they may not understand."[22] Those who are now waiting to see the issue of this work think they shall be better able to determine its reality by and by. Probably many of them are mistaken. The Jews saw Christ's miracles and waited to see better evidences of His being the Messiah. They wanted a sign from heaven; but they waited in vain. Their stumbling blocks did not diminish but increased. They found no end to them and so were more and more hardened in unbelief. Many have been praying for that glorious reformation spoken of in Scripture, not knowing what they have been praying for. If it should come, they would not acknowledge or receive it. It was this way with the Jews when they prayed for the coming of Christ.

By this they miss sharing the great blessing. They also miss the most precious opportunity of obtaining the most heavenly eternal benefits that God ever gave in New England—His divine light, grace, and comfort. The glorious fountain is set open in so wonderful a manner, and multitudes flock to it and receive a rich supply for the needs of their souls. These excessively cautious ones stand at a distance, doubting, wondering, and receiving nothing. They will probably continue to hesitate till the precious season is past. The credibility of those who doubt the work is to be challenged! Uncommon external appearances have accompanied the work. Yet these skeptics are so easy in their doubts. They make no effort to inform themselves. They do not go where they can closely observe and diligently inquire into the work. They are content with observing two or three instances. They make no effort to be fully informed by their own observation. I am sure that if they had thoroughly examined the evidence, it would have convinced them, unless their minds are closed to persuasion. How greatly have they erred who only from the uncertain reproofs of others speak slightly of these things. The caution of an unbelieving Jew might teach them more discretion.[23]

Is what has been said in this discourse enough to produce conviction that this is the work of God? Even if it is not, I hope that for the future they will at least listen to the caution of Gamaliel. I hope they will not oppose this work of God or endorse anything that has even an indirect tendency to bring it into discredit. If they do, they may be found to be opposers of the Holy Spirit.

There is no kind of sin so hurtful and dangerous to the souls of men as that committed against the Holy Spirit. We had better speak against God the Father or the Son than to speak against the Holy Spirit in His gracious operations on the hearts of men. Nothing else will so much tend forever to prevent our having any benefit of His operations on our own souls.

Are there any who still intently speak with disdain of these things? I beg of them to take heed that they be not guilty of the unpardonable sin. When is the most likely time for this sin to be committed? When the Holy Spirit is greatly poured out and men's lusts, lukewarmness, and hypocrisy are reproached by His powerful operations. If the work goes on, I hope that among the many who oppose it some are not guilty of this sin—if none have been already. Some maliciously oppose and reproach this work by calling it the work of the devil. They lack but one thing of the unpardonable sin, and that is doing it against inward conviction. Some are wise enough not to openly oppose and reproach this work. Yet this is to be feared. Today the Lord is going forth so gloriously against His enemies. Many who are silent and inactive, especially ministers, will bring that curse of the angel of the Lord upon themselves: "'Curse Meron,' said the angel of the Lord, 'Curse its people bitterly, because they did not come to help the LORD, to help the LORD against the mighty.'"[24]

The great God has come down from heaven. He has manifested Himself in so wonderful a manner in this land. Therefore, it is vain for any of us to expect not to be greatly affected by it in our spiritual state and circumstances. It affects the favor of God one way or the other. Those who do not become happier by it will become far more guilty and miserable. It is always so. Such a season is a time of great favor to those who accept and improve. But when God comes down, it proves a day of vengeance to others.[25] When God sends forth His Word, it shall not return to Him void.[26] Much less His Spirit! When Christ was upon earth in Judea, many slighted and rejected Him. But they could not be indifferent to Him. God made all those people feel that Christ had been among them. Those who did not feel it to their comfort felt it to their great sorrow. God sent the prophet Ezekiel alone to the children of Israel. Then He declared that whether they would hear or whether they would ignore, yet they would know there had been a prophet among them.[27] How much more may we suppose that when God has appeared so wonderfully in this land, He will make everyone know that the great Jehovah has been in New England.

I come now, in the last place, to the friends of this work.

III. Friends of This Work Must Give Diligent Heed to Themselves

I speak now to those who are the friends of this work, who have been partakers of it and are zealous to promote it. Let me earnestly exhort such to give diligent heed to themselves. Avoid all errors and misconduct. Avoid whatever may darken and obscure the work. Give no occasion to those who stand ready to reproach it. The apostle Paul was careful to give no such occasion to those who desired it. The same apostle exhorted Titus to maintain a strict care and watch over himself, that both his preaching and behavior might be such as "cannot be condemned, so that those who oppose you may be ashamed because they have nothing bad to say about us."[28] We have need to be wise as serpents and harmless as doves. It is of no small consequence that we must at this day behave ourselves innocently and prudently. We must expect that the great enemy of this work will especially try his utmost with us. He will especially triumph if he can prevail in any way to blind and mislead us. We need to watch and pray, for we are but little children. This roaring lion is too strong for us. This old serpent is too subtle for us.[29]

Humility and self-denial and an entire dependence on our Lord Jesus Christ will be our best defense. Let us therefore maintain the strictest watch against spiritual pride. Let us avoid being lifted up with extraordinary experiences and comforts. Let us not take pride in the high favors of heaven that any of us may have received. We need these favors in a special manner in order to keep a strict and jealous eye upon our own hearts. Otherwise, there should arise self-exalting reflections upon what we have received. We would have high thoughts of ourselves as being now some of the most eminent of saints and special favorites of heaven. We would think that the secret of the Lord is especially with us. Let us not presume that we above all are fit to be advanced as the great instructors and censors of this evil generation. Let us not in a high conceit of our own wisdom and discernment assume ourselves to be the heirs of prophets or extraordinary ambassadors of heaven. When we have great discoveries of God made to our souls, we should not shine bright in our own eyes. When Moses conversed with God on the mount, his face shone so as to dazzle the eyes of Aaron and the people. Yet he did not shine in his own eyes. "He was not aware that his face was radiant."[30]

> **Pride is the worst viper in the heart. It is the first sin that ever entered into the universe. It lies lowest of all in the foundation of the whole building of sin. Of all lusts, it is the most secret, deceitful, and unsearchable in its ways of working. It is ready to mix with everything. Nothing is so hateful to God, contrary to the spirit of the Gospel, or of so dangerous consequence. There is no one sin that does so much to let the devil into the hearts of the saints and expose them to his delusions.**

Let none think themselves out of danger of this spiritual pride, even on their best day. God saw that the apostle Paul (though probably the most eminent saint who ever lived) was not out of danger of it, not when he had just been conversing with God in the third heaven.[31] Pride is the worst viper in the heart. It is the first sin that ever entered into the universe. It lies lowest of all in the foundation of the whole building of sin. Of all lusts, it is the most secret, deceitful, and unsearchable in its ways of working. It is ready to mix with everything. Nothing is so hateful to God, contrary to the spirit of the Gospel, or of so dangerous consequence. There is no one sin that does so much to let the devil into the hearts of the saints and expose them to his delusions. I have seen it in many instances in highly respected saints. The devil enters the door of pride after some eminent experience and extraordinary communion with God. He woefully deludes and leads astray till God has mercifully opened their eyes and delivered them. They themselves have afterwards been made aware that it was pride that betrayed them.

Some of the true friends of the work of God's Spirit have

erred in giving too much heed to impulses and strong impressions on their minds. They act as though these ideas were direct messages from heaven to them. These messages deal with something that will come to pass or something that was the mind and will of God that they should do. These messages were not signified or revealed anywhere in the Bible apart from those impulses. These ideas, if they are truly from the Spirit of God, are very different from His gracious influences on the hearts of the saints. They are extraordinary gifts of the Spirit that are properly inspired, such as the prophets and apostles and others had of old. The apostle distinguishes these extraordinary gifts from the grace of the Spirit.[32]

The blessed image of God consists in saving grace and not in miraculous gifts.

One reason some trust such impulses is an opinion they have had. They believe the glory of the approaching happy days of the church will partly consist in restoring those extraordinary gifts of the Spirit. This opinion, I believe, arises partly through not duly considering and comparing the nature and value of those two kinds of influences of the Spirit. One kind is ordinary and gracious. The other kind is extraordinary and miraculous. The ordinary and gracious are by far the most excellent and glorious, as the apostle largely shows. Speaking of the extraordinary gifts of the Spirit, he says, "But eagerly desire the greater gifts. And now I will show you the most excellent way,"[33] that is, a more excellent way of the influence of the Spirit. And then he goes on in the next chapter to show what that more excellent way is. It is the grace of the Spirit, which concisely consists in divine love. And throughout that chapter the apostle shows the great preference of that above inspiration.

God communicates His own nature to the soul in saving grace in the heart more than in all miraculous gifts. The blessed image of God consists in saving grace and not in miraculous gifts. The excellency, happiness, and glory of the soul immediately consists in the ordinary and gracious—that is, a root that bears infinitely more excellent fruit. Salvation and the eternal enjoyment of God is associated with divine grace but not with inspiration. A man may have the extraordinary gifts, yet be abominable to God and go to hell. The spiritual and eternal life of the soul consists in the grace of the Spirit that God bestows only on His favorite and dear children. He has sometimes thrown out the other, as it were, to dogs and swine, as He did to Balaam, Saul, and Judas[34] and some who in the first times of the Christian church committed the unpardonable sin.[35] Many wicked men at the day of judgment will plead, "Lord, Lord, did we not prophesy in your name, and in your name drive out demons and perform many miracles?"[36] The greatest privilege of the prophets and apostles was not their being inspired and working miracles but their eminent holiness. The grace that was in their hearts was a thousand times more their dignity and honor than their miraculous gifts. David comforted himself not because he was a king or a prophet. He comforted himself because of the Holy Spirit's influences in his heart. These influences communicated to him divine light, love, and joy.

The apostle Paul abounded in visions, revelations, and miraculous gifts above all the apostles. Yet he esteemed all things but loss for the excellency of the spiritual knowledge of Christ. It was not the gifts but the grace of the apostles that was the proper evidence of their names being written in heaven; in which Christ directed them to rejoice much more than in the devils being subject to them.[37] To have grace in the heart is a higher privilege than the blessed Virgin herself had in having the body of the second person of the Trinity conceived in her womb by the power of the Highest overshadowing her. "As Jesus was saying these things, a woman in the crowd called out, 'Blessed is the mother who gave you birth and nursed you.' He replied, 'Blessed rather are those who hear the word of God and obey it.'"[38] The influence of the Holy Spirit, divine love in the heart, is a greater privilege and glory than is experienced by the highest archangel in heaven. Yes, this is the very thing by which the creature has fellowship with God Himself, with the Father and the Son in their beauty and happiness. By this influence of the Spirit, the saints are made partakers of the divine nature and have Christ's joy fulfilled in themselves.

The greatest privilege of the prophets and apostles was not their being inspired and working miracles but their eminent holiness. . . . The extraordinary gifts are worthless without the ordinary sanctifying influences.

The ordinary sanctifying influences of the Spirit of God are the objective of all extraordinary gifts, as the apostle shows.[39] They are good for nothing unless they are subject to this end. The extraordinary gifts are worthless without the ordinary sanctifying influences. The first without the second will only aggravate men's misery. This is, as the apostle observes, the most excellent way of God's communicating His Spirit to His Church. It is the greatest glory of the Church in all ages. This glory is what makes the Church on earth most like the Church in heaven, where prophecy and tongues and other miraculous gifts cease. And God communicates His Spirit only in that more excellent way of which the apostle speaks—divine love that "never fails." Therefore, the glory of the approaching happy state of the Church does not at all require these extraordinary gifts. That state of the Church will be the nearest of any to its perfect state in heaven. I believe it will be like it in this way: All extraordinary gifts shall have ceased and vanished away. And all those stars and the moon, with the reflected light they gave in the night or in a dark season, shall be swallowed up in the sun of divine love. The apostle speaks of these gifts of inspiration as childish things in comparison to the influence of the Spirit in divine love. They are given to the Church only to support it in its infancy. When the Church should have a complete standing rule established and all the ordinary means of grace are settled, these gifts should cease as the church advances to the state of manhood. "When I was a child, I talked like a child, I thought like a child, I reasoned like a child. When I became a man, I put childish ways behind me."[40]

The apostle, in this chapter, speaks of prophecies, tongues, and revelations ceasing and vanishing from the church. The Christian church should advance from minority to manhood. Paul seems to be referring to the church coming to an adult state in this world as well as in heaven. He speaks of such a state of manhood in which these three things—faith, hope, and love—should remain after miracles and revelations have ceased, as in the last verse: "Now these three remain: faith, hope, and love." The apostle's manner of speaking here shows an obvious reference to what he had just been saying. Here is an obvious contrast between remaining and that failing, ceasing, and vanishing away spoken of in verse 8. All those gifts of inspiration were the leading strings of the Christian church in its infancy. The apostle had been showing how all those gifts of inspiration should vanish away when the church came to a state of manhood. Then he returns to observe what things remain after those had failed and ceased. And he observes that those three things shall remain in the Church—faith, hope, and love. Therefore, the adult state of the Church he speaks of is the more perfect one at which it shall arrive on earth, especially in the latter ages of the world. And this was more properly stated to the church at Corinth upon two accounts—because he had before told that church they were in a state of infancy[41] and because that church seemed above all others to abound with miraculous gifts. When the expected glorious state of the church comes, the increase of light shall be so great that it will in some respects answer what is said of seeing face to face.[42]

Therefore, I do not expect a restoration of these miraculous gifts in the approaching glorious times of the Church, nor do I desire it. It appears to me that it would add nothing to the glory of those times but rather diminish from it. For my part, I had rather enjoy the sweet influences of the Spirit. I had rather show Christ's spiritual divine beauty, infinite grace, and dying love. I had rather draw forth the holy exercises of faith, divine love, sweet complacence, and humble joy in God. I had rather experience all this for one quarter of an hour than to have prophetical visions and revelations the whole year. It appears to me much more probable that God should give immediate revelations to His saints in the dark times of prophecy than now in the approaching most glorious and perfect state of His church on earth. I do not think there is any need of those extraordinary gifts to introduce this happy state and set up the kingdom of God throughout the world. I have seen so much of the power of God in a more excellent way as to convince me that God can easily do it without extraordinary gifts.

I would therefore appeal to the people of God to be very cautious how they give heed to such extraordinary gifts. I have seen them fail in very many instances. I know by experience that impressions made with great power upon the minds of true and eminent saints are no sure signs of their being revelations from heaven. This is true even in the midst of extraordinary expressions of grace and sweet communion with God attended with texts of Scripture strongly impressed on the mind. I have known such impressions to fail. In some instances they failed even when all these circumstances are present. God has given us the sure word of prophecy as a light shining in a dark place. They who leave that word to follow such impressions and impulses leave the guidance of the polar star to follow a man with a lamp. No wonder, therefore, that sometimes they are led into woeful extravagances.

Moreover, since inspiration is not to be expected, let us not despise human learning. They who assert that human learning is of little or no use in the work of the ministry do not well consider what they say. If they did, they would not say it. By human learning I mean, and suppose others mean, the improvement of common knowledge by human and outward means. To say that human learning is of no use is to say that the education of a child is useless, that the common knowledge of a grown man is of no more value than that of a little child. If this is true, a four-year-old child is as fit to be a teacher in the church of God as a very knowing man of thirty years of age. All the child needs is the same degree of grace to be capable of doing as much to advance the kingdom of Christ by his instruction. But adults have greater ability and advantage to do service because they have more knowledge than a little child. Then without a doubt, if they have more human knowledge with the same degree of grace, they would have greater ability and advantage to do service. An increase of knowledge without doubt increases a man's advantage either to do good or harm, according to how he is disposed. It cannot be denied that God made great use of human learning in the apostle Paul, as He also did in Moses and Solomon.

Study is the means of obtaining knowledge. So if we are not to despise knowledge obtained by human means, then it will follow that we are not to neglect study. Furthermore, study is of great use to prepare for publicly instructing others. And though having the heart full of the powerful influences of the Spirit of God may at some time enable persons to speak profitably and very excellently without study, this possibility will not warrant us needlessly to cast ourselves down from the pinnacle of the temple. We should not depend upon the angel of the Lord to bear us up. He will not keep us from dashing our foot against a stone when there is another way to go down, though the other way may not be so quick. I would pray that the method in public discourses that tends greatly to help both the understanding and memory may not be wholly neglected.

I beg the dear children of God more fully to consider one other thing: How far do the rules of the Holy Scriptures truly justify their passing censures upon other professing Christians? Upon what grounds do they judge people to be hypocrites and ignorant of real Christian faith? We all know that there is a judging and censuring of some sort or other that the Scripture very often and very strictly forbids. Look into those rules of Scripture. Thoroughly weigh them. Consider whether our taking it upon us to discern the state of others is not really forbidden by Christ in the New Testament. We are not to pass sentence upon them as wicked men. They are professing Christians and of a good visible conduct. The disciples of Christ ought to avoid this practice. They may think themselves sufficient for it. They may think it a needful and good tendency. It is plain that the sort of judgment that God claims as His prerogative, whatever that be, is forbidden. We know that a certain judging of the hearts of the children of men is often spoken of as the great prerogative of God. This belongs only to Him. As Scripture says, "Forgive and act; deal with each man according to all he does, since you know his heart (for you alone know the hearts of all men)."[43] If we examine this matter, we shall find this: The judging of hearts that is spoken of as God's prerogative relates to the aims and dispositions of men's hearts in particular actions. But God primarily judges their hearts concerning their profession of Christian faith. This appears very obvious by looking over many Scriptures.[44]

The sort of judging that is God's proper business is forbidden. "Who are you to judge someone else's servant? To his own master he stands or falls."[45] "There is only one Lawgiver and Judge, the One who is able to save and destroy. But you—who are you to judge your neighbor?[46] "I care very little if I am judged by you or by any human court; indeed, I do not even judge myself. My conscience is clear, but that does not make me innocent. It is the Lord who judges me."[47]

Again, whatever kind of judging is the proper work and business of the day of judgment, we are forbidden. "Therefore, judge nothing before the appointed time; wait till the Lord comes. He will bring to light what is hidden in darkness and will expose the motives of men's hearts. At that time each will receive his praise from God."[48] It is the proper business of the day of judgment to distinguish hypocrites with only the form of godliness and the visible conduct of godly men from the true saints. Then God will separate the sheep from the goats. Yes, this is represented as the main business and end of that day. They, therefore, do greatly err who take it upon them to determine absolutely who are sincere and who are not. They cannot draw the dividing line between true saints and hypocrites. They cannot separate between sheep and goats, setting the one on the right hand and the other on the left.[49] They cannot distinguish and gather out the tares from among the wheat. Many of the servants of the owner of the field are very ready to think themselves sufficient for this. They are confident to offer their service to this end. But their Lord says, "No, because while you are pulling the weeds, you may root up the wheat with them. Let both grow together until the harvest. At that time I will tell the harvesters . . ." In the time of harvest, their Lord will take care to see a thorough separation made.[50] This agrees with the previously mentioned prohibition of the apostle: "judge nothing before the appointed time."[51]

In this parable, the servants who have the care of the fruit of the field are the same servants who elsewhere have the care of the fruit of the vineyard. They are represented as servants of the Lord of the harvest. He appointed them as laborers in His harvest.[52] These we know are the ministers of the Gospel. Now is that parable fulfilled: "While everyone was sleeping [during a long sleepy, dead time in the church], his enemy came and sowed weeds." Now is the time "when the wheat sprouted and formed heads," and the Christian faith is reviving. And now some of the servants who have the care of the field say, "Do you want us to go and pull them up?"[53] This is a great tendency in men who suppose they have had some experience of the power of the Christian faith. They think they are able to discern and determine the state of others by a little conversation with them. Experience has taught me that this is an error. There was a time when I did not imagine that the heart of man was so unsearchable as it is. I am less tolerant and less intolerant than once I was. I find more things in wicked men that may be counterfeit, even when they make a fair show of piety. I find more ways that the remaining corruption of the godly may make them appear like carnal men, formalists, and dead hypocrites than once I knew of. The longer I live, the less I wonder that God keeps it as His right to try the hearts of the children of men. Also I wonder less that God directs that this business should be let alone till harvest. I adore the wisdom of God! In His goodness to me and my fellow creatures, He has not committed this great business into our hands. We are such poor, weak, and dim-sighted creatures. We are so blind, full of pride, partial, prejudiced, and deceitful of heart. So He has committed it into the hands of One infinitely fitter for it and has made it His own right.

> The longer I live, the less I wonder that God keeps it as His right to try the hearts of the children of men. Also I wonder less that God directs that this business should be let alone till harvest. I adore the wisdom of God! In His goodness to me and my fellow creatures, He has not committed this great business into our hands. We are such poor, weak, and dim-sighted creatures. We are so blind, full of pride, partial, prejudiced, and deceitful of heart. So He has committed it into the hands of One infinitely fitter for it and has made it His own right.

The talk of some persons and the account they give of their experiences is exceedingly satisfying. It forbids and banishes the thought of them being any other than the precious children of God. It obliges and, as it were, forces full love. But yet we must allow the Scriptures to stand true that speak of everything in the saint belonging to the spiritual and divine life as hidden.[54] Their food is the hidden manna. They have meat to eat that others know not of. A stranger does not mingle with their joys. The heart in which they possess their divine distinguishing ornaments is the hidden man. Only God sees it.[55] Their new name, which Christ has given them, no man knows but he that receives it.[56]

The true Israelites are those whose circumcision is by God, of the heart, and not of men.[57] They can be known for certain to be Israelites and have the honor that belongs to such. This honor comes only from God. This appears by the use of a similar expression by the same apostle. He speaks of its being God's prerogative to judge who are upright Christians and what He will do at the day of judgment, adding. "At that time each will receive his praise from God."[58]

The instance of Judas is remarkable. He was with the rest of the disciples, who were all persons of true experience. His associates never seemed to entertain a thought that he was anything but a true disciple till he showed himself by his scandalous acts. And the instance of Ahithophel is also very remarkable. Though David was a wise and holy man, a great king, a divine, and had a great acquaintance with Scripture, he did not suspect him. David knew more than all his teachers, more than the ancients. He had grown old in experience and was in the greatest ripeness of his judgment. He was a great prophet and was intimately acquainted with Ahithophel.[59] Ahithophel was his familiar friend and most intimate companion in religious and spiritual concerns. Yet David never discovered him to be a hypocrite but relied upon him as a true saint. David relished that man's religious teaching—it was sweet to him. He counted Ahithophel an eminent saint. He made him, above any other man, his guide and counselor in spiritual matters. Yet Ahithophel was not only *not* a saint but was a notoriously wicked man. He was a murderous, vile wretch. Thus David says, "Destructive forces are at work in the city; threats and lies never leave its streets. If an [open] enemy were insulting me, I could endure it; if a foe were raising himself against me, I could hide from him. But it is you, a man like myself, my companion, my close friend, with whom I once enjoyed sweet fellowship as we walked with the throng at the house of God" (Psalm 55:11-14).

To suppose that men have the ability and right to determine the state of the souls of visible Christians carries in it an inconsistency. Men cannot make an open separation between saints and hypocrites. True saints are not of one visible company and hypocrites of another, separated by a partition that men make. This supposes that God has given men power to make another visible church within his visible church. By the term visible Christians or visible saints is meant persons who have a right to be received as such in the eye of public goodwill. God has established a regular ecclesiastical proceeding for discipline in His visible church. I beg those who have a true zeal for promoting the work of God well to consider these things. Some do not listen to me now. But I am persuaded that those who have much to do with souls will be of the same mind when they have had more experience.

There is another thing I entreat the zealous friends of this glorious work of God to avoid. Manage the controversy with opposers with less heat and appearance of an angry zeal. I especially urge very much public prayer and preaching on the persecution of opposers. If their persecution were ten times greater than it is, I think it would not be good to say so much about it. It is proper for Christians to be like lambs who are not apt to complain and cry when they are hurt. It becomes Christians to be dumb and not to open their mouths, after the example of our dear Redeemer.[60] We are not to be like swine that are apt to scream aloud when they are touched. We should not be quick to think and speak of fire from heaven when the Samaritans oppose us and will not receive us into their villages.[61] God's zealous ministers would do well to think of the direction the apostle Paul gave to a zealous minister: "The Lord's servant must not quarrel; instead, he must be kind to everyone, able to teach, not resentful. Those who oppose him he must gently instruct, in the hope that God will grant them repentance leading them to a knowledge of the truth, and that they will come to their senses and escape from the trap of the devil, who has taken them captive to do his will" (2 Timothy 2:24-26).

Do you love the Lord Jesus Christ and desire to advance His kingdom? I would humbly recommend that you give close attention to that excellent rule of prudence that Christ has left us: "No one sews a patch of unshrunk cloth on an old garment, for the patch will pull away from the garment, making the tear worse. Neither do men pour new wine into old wineskins. If they do, the skins will burst, the wine will run out and the wineskins will be ruined. No, they pour new wine into new wineskins, and both are preserved" (Matthew 9:16-17). I am afraid the wine is now running out in some part of this land for lack of obeying this rule. I believe we have confined ourselves too much to a certain stated method and form in the management of our religious affairs. This has tended to cause all our Christian faith to degenerate into mere formality. Whatever has the appearance of a great innovation tends greatly to hinder the progress of the power of the Christian faith. These innovations tend to greatly shock and surprise people's minds. They set people talking and disputing. They raise the opposition of some and divert the minds of others. These innovations perplex many with doubts and scruples. They cause people to swerve from their great business and turn aside to vain jangling. Therefore, these great innovations, unless they are of considerable importance, are best avoided.

In this we must follow the example of one who had the greatest success in spreading the power of the Christian faith: "To the Jews I became like a Jew, to win the Jews. To those under the law I became like one under the law (though I myself am not under the law), so as to win those under the law. To those not having the law I became like one not having the law (though I am not free from God's law but am under Christ's law), so as to win those not having the law. To the weak I became weak, to win the weak. I have become all things to all men so that by all possible means I might save some. I do all this for the sake of the gospel, that I may share in its blessings" (1 Corinthians 9:20-23).

FOOTNOTES TO THIS SECTION

1. Five points of deist belief are: (1) the existence of a personal God who was Creator and Ruler of the universe; (2) the obligation of divine worship; (3) the necessity of ethical conduct; (4) the necessity of repentance from sin; (5) divine rewards and punishments here and in the life of the soul after death. Negatively, the Deists denied any intervention of God in the natural order in the past. They acknowledged general providence but denied the Trinity, the Incarnation, the divine authority of the Bible, the Atonement, miracles, any particular elect people such as Israel or the Church, or any supernatural redemptive acts in history.

2. Mark 1:26. See also Mark 9:26.

3. Genesis 1:3.

4. "It was because you, the Levites, did not bring it up the first time that the LORD our God broke out in anger against us. We did not inquire of him about how to do it in the prescribed way" (1 Chronicles 15:13).

5. "One day the angels came to present themselves before the LORD, and Satan also came with them" (Job 1:6).

6. "The king had a fleet of trading ships at sea along with the ships of Hiram. Once every three years it returned carrying gold, silver and ivory, and apes and baboons" (1 Kings 10:22). "The king had a fleet of trading ships manned by Hiram's men. Once every three years it returned carrying gold, silver and ivory, and apes and baboons" (2 Chronicles 9:21b).

7. Mark 4:26-28.

8. "Serve the LORD with fear and rejoice with trembling" (Psalm 2:11).

9. Genesis 28:12-17.

10. Exodus 34:8.

11. See John 1:11.

12. Isaiah 29:14.

13. "But we preach Christ crucified: a stumbling block to Jews and foolishness to Gentiles, but to those whom God has called, both Jews and Greeks, Christ the power of God and the wisdom of God" (1 Corinthians 1:23).

14. Matthew 11:6.

15. Luke 12:56-57.

16. Matthew 12:30; Luke 11:23.

17. Acts 13:40-41.

18. 2 Kings 7:2.

19. Matthew 18:7.

20. "We preach Christ crucified: a stumbling block to Jews and foolishness to Gentiles" (1 Corinthians 1:23).

21. Hosea 14:9.

22. Luke 8:10.

23. "Therefore, in the present case I advise you: Leave these men alone! Let them go! For if their purpose or activity is of human origin, it will fail. But if it is from God, you will not be able to stop these men; you will only find yourselves fighting against God" (Acts 5:38).

24. Judges 5:23.

25. "To proclaim the year of the LORD's favor and the day of vengeance of our God, to comfort all who mourn" (Isaiah 61:2).

26. "So is my word that goes out from my mouth: It will not return to me empty, but will accomplish what I desire and achieve the purpose for which I sent it" (Isaiah 55:11).

27. Ezekiel 2:5.

28. Titus 2:7-8.

29. "Be self-controlled and alert. Your enemy the devil prowls around like a roaring lion looking for someone to devour" (1 Peter 5:8). "Now the serpent was more crafty than any of the wild animals the LORD God had made. He said to the woman, 'Did God really say, "You must not eat from any tree in the garden?"' The woman said to the serpent, 'We may eat fruit from the trees in the garden, but God did say, "You must not eat fruit from the tree that is in the middle of the garden, and you must not touch it, or you will die."' 'You will not surely die,' the serpent said to the woman. 'For God knows that when you eat of it your eyes will be opened, and you will be like God, knowing good and evil'" (Genesis 3:1-5). "Then the LORD God said to the woman, 'What is this you have done?' The woman said, 'The serpent deceived me, and I ate'" (Genesis 3:13). "The great dragon was hurled down—that ancient serpent called the devil or Satan, who leads the whole world astray. He was hurled to the earth, and his angels with him" (Revelation 12:9).

30. "When Moses came down from Mount Sinai with the two tablets of the Testimony in his hands, he was not aware that his face was radiant because he had spoken with the LORD. When Aaron and all the Israelites saw Moses, his face was radiant, and they were afraid to come near him" (Exodus 34:29-30). "They saw that his face was radiant. Then Moses would put the veil back over his face until he went in to speak with the LORD" (Exodus 34:35).

31. "To keep me from becoming conceited because of these surpassingly great

revelations, there was given me a thorn in my flesh, a messenger of Satan, to torment me" (2 Corinthians 12:7).

32. "If I speak in the tongues of men and of angels, but have not love, I am only a resounding gong or a clanging cymbal. If I have the gift of prophecy and can fathom all mysteries and all knowledge, and if I have a faith that can move mountains, but have not love, I am nothing. If I give all I possess to the poor and surrender my body to the flames, but have not love, I gain nothing. Love is patient, love is kind. It does not envy, it does not boast, it is not proud. It is not rude, it is not self-seeking, it is not easily angered, it keeps no record of wrongs. Love does not delight in evil but rejoices with the truth. It always protects, always trusts, always hopes, always perseveres. Love never fails. But where there are prophecies, they will cease; where there are tongues, they will be stilled; where there is knowledge, it will pass away. For we know in part and we prophesy in part. But when perfection comes, the imperfect disappears. When I was a child, I talked like a child, I thought like a child, I reasoned like a child. When I became a man, I put childish ways behind me. Now we see but a poor reflection; then we shall see face to face. Now I know in part; then I shall know fully, even as I am fully known. And now these three remain: faith, hope and love. But the greatest of these is love" (1 Corinthians 13:1-13).

33. 1 Corinthians 12:31.

34. Balaam—see Numbers 22—24; Saul—see 1 Samuel 10:10-11; Judas, numbered with the Twelve—see Matthew 10:2-5. "These twelve Jesus sent out with the following instructions: 'Do not go among the Gentiles or enter any town of the Samaritans. Go rather to the lost sheep of Israel. As you go, preach this message: "The kingdom of heaven is near." Heal the sick, raise the dead, cleanse those who have leprosy, drive out demons. Freely you have received, freely give'" (Matt. 10:5-8).

35. "Therefore, let us leave the elementary teachings about Christ and go on to maturity, not laying again the foundation of repentance from acts that lead to death, and of faith in God, instruction about baptisms, the laying on of hands, the resurrection of the dead, and eternal judgment. And God permitting, we will do so. It is impossible for those who have once been enlightened, who have tasted the heavenly gift, who have shared in the Holy Spirit, who have tasted the goodness of the word of God and the powers of the coming age, if they fall away, to be brought back to repentance, because to their loss they are crucifying the Son of God all over again and subjecting him to public disgrace" (Hebrews 6:1-6).

36. Matthew 7:22.

37. Luke 10:20.

38. Luke 11:27-28; Matthew 12:47.

39. "It was he who gave some to be apostles, some to be prophets, some to be evangelists, and some to be pastors and teachers, to prepare God's people for works of service, so that the body of Christ may be built up until we all reach unity in the faith and in the knowledge of the Son of God and become

mature, attaining to the whole measure of the fullness of Christ" (Ephesians 4:11-13).

40. 1 Corinthians 13:11.

41. "Brothers, I could not address you as spiritual but as worldly—mere infants in Christ. I gave you milk, not solid food, for you were not yet ready for it. Indeed, you are still not ready" (1 Corinthians 3:1-2).

42. "Now we see but a poor reflection; then we shall see face to face. Now I know in part; then I shall know fully, even as I am fully known" (1 Corinthians 13:12). See Isaiah 24:23. "The moon will be abashed, the sun ashamed; for the Lord Almighty will reign on Mount Zion and in Jerusalem, and before its elders, gloriously. On this mountain He will destroy the shroud that enfolds all peoples, the sheet that covers all nations" (Isaiah 25:7).

43. 1 Kings 8:39.

44. "And you, my son Solomon, acknowledge the God of your father, and serve him with wholehearted devotion and with a willing mind, for the LORD searches every heart and understands every motive behind the thoughts. If you seek him, he will be found by you; but if you forsake him, he will reject you forever" (1 Chronicles 28:9). "O righteous God, who searches minds and hearts, bring to an end the violence of the wicked and make the righteous secure. My shield is God Most High, who saves the upright in heart. God is a righteous judge, a God who expresses his wrath every day" (Psalm 7:9-11). "Vindicate me, O LORD, for I have led a blameless life; I have trusted in the LORD without wavering. Test me, O LORD, and try me, examine my heart and my mind; for your love is ever before me, and I walk continually in your truth. I do not sit with deceitful men, nor do I consort with hypocrites; I abhor the assembly of evildoers and refuse to sit with the wicked. I wash my hands in innocence, and go about Your altar, O LORD, proclaiming aloud your praise and telling of all your wonderful deeds. I love the house where You live, O LORD, the place where your glory dwells. Do not take away my soul along with sinners or my life with bloodthirsty men, in whose hands are wicked schemes, whose right hands are full of bribes. But I lead a blameless life; redeem me and be merciful to me. My feet stand on level ground; in the great assembly I will praise the LORD" (Psalm 26:1-12). "All a man's ways seem innocent to him, but motives are weighed by the LORD" (Proverbs 16:2). "All a man's ways seem right to him, but the LORD weighs the heart" (Proverbs 21:2). "Now while He was in Jerusalem at the Passover Feast, many people saw the miraculous signs he was doing and believed in his name. But Jesus would not entrust himself to them, for he knew all men. He did not need man's testimony about man, for he knew what was in a man" (John 2:23). "So I will cast her on a bed of suffering, and I will make those who commit adultery with her suffer intensely, unless they repent of her ways. I will strike her children dead. Then all the churches will know that I am He who searches hearts and minds, and I will repay each of you according to your deeds" (Revelation 2:22).

45. Romans 14:4.

46. James 4:12.

47. 1 Corinthians 4:3-4.

48. 1 Corinthians 4:5.

49. "All the nations will be gathered before him, and he will separate the people one from another as a shepherd separates the sheep from the goats. He will put the sheep on his right and the goats on his left" (Matthew 25:32).

50. "'An enemy did this,' he replied. The servants asked him, 'Do you want us to go and pull them up?' 'No,' he answered, 'because while you are pulling the weeds, you may root up the wheat with them. Let both grow together until the harvest. At that time I will tell the harvesters: First collect the weeds and tie them in bundles to be burned; then gather the wheat and bring it into my barn'" (Matthew 13:28-30).

51. 1 Corinthians 4:5.

52. "He went on to tell the people this parable: 'A man planted a vineyard, rented it to some farmers and went away for a long time. At harvest time he sent a servant to the tenants so they would give him some of the fruit of the vineyard. But the tenants beat him and sent him away empty-handed. He sent another servant, but that one also they beat and treated shamefully and sent away empty-handed. He sent still a third, and they wounded him and threw him out. Then the owner of the vineyard said, "What shall I do? I will send my son, whom I love; perhaps they will respect him." But when the tenants saw him, they talked the matter over. "This is the heir," they said. "Let's kill him, and the inheritance will be ours." So they threw him out of the vineyard and killed him. What then will the owner of the vineyard do to them? He will come and kill those tenants and give the vineyard to others.' When the people heard this, they said, 'May this never be!'" (Luke 20:9-16).

53. "Jesus told them another parable: 'The kingdom of heaven is like a man who sowed good seed in his field. But while everyone was sleeping, his enemy came and sowed weeds among the wheat, and went away. When the wheat sprouted and formed heads, then the weeds also appeared. The owner's servants came to him and said, "Sir, didn't you sow good seed in your field? Where then did the weeds come from?" "An enemy did this," he replied. The servants asked him, "Do you want us to go and pull them up?" "No," he answered, "because while you are pulling the weeds, you may root up the wheat with them. Let both grow together until the harvest. At that time I will tell the harvesters: First collect the weeds and tie them in bundles to be burned; then gather the wheat and bring it into my barn'" (Matthew 13:24-30).

54. "For you died, and your life is now hidden with Christ in God. When Christ, who is your life, appears, then you also will appear with him in glory" (Colossians 3:3-4).

55. "Instead, it should be that of your inner self, the unfading beauty of a gentle and quiet spirit, which is of great worth in God's sight" (1 Peter 3:4).

56. "He who has an ear, let him hear what the Spirit says to the churches. To him who overcomes, I will give some of the hidden manna. I will also give

him a white stone with a new name written on it, known only to him who receives it" (Revelation 2:17).

57. "No, a man is a Jew if he is one inwardly; and circumcision is circumcision of the heart, by the Spirit, not by the written code. Such a man's praise is not from men, but from God" (Romans 2:29).

58. "Therefore, judge nothing before the appointed time; wait till the Lord comes. He will bring to light what is hidden in darkness and will expose the motives of men's hearts" (1 Corinthians 4:5).

59. "Now in those days the advice Ahithophel gave was like that of one who inquires of God. That was how both David and Absalom regarded all of Ahithophel's advice" (2 Samuel 16:23). To get the whole picture of this relationship, read 1 Samuel 15—17.

60. "He was oppressed and afflicted, yet he did not open his mouth; he was led like a lamb to the slaughter, and as a sheep before her shearers is silent, so he did not open his mouth" (Isaiah 53:7).

61. "When the disciples James and John saw this, they asked, 'Lord, do you want us to call fire down from heaven to destroy them?'" (Luke 9:54).

EPILOGUE

APPENDIX

DISCUSSION GUIDE

SESSION AGENDAS

EPILOGUE

Prepare the Way for the Lord

As we have seen, to be revived is to wake up and live! It is like a prairie fire ignited by lightning bolts from heaven. In the Great Awakening we saw that revival is in every way supernatural and extraordinary. Vast numbers of people of all ages and all ranks and degrees were transformed. They were ignorant and learned. Some were crude and disorderly; others were the worst possible sinners, sensual worldlings. Those who once treated this work with contempt became its champions. Many who merely professed formal religion suddenly expressed deep passionate love for God.

Revival is a God-wrought transformation in the inner person that reaches into the total fabric of life and culture. It appears when the Body of Christ, the Church, is at the brink of death. The heart is beating its last, and so God Himself takes direct action. Like a divine emergency-room doctor, the Holy Spirit applies supernatural CPR, breathing the fresh air of heaven into the lungs of the Church. He massages the heart until there is again a strong, healthy heartbeat. Revival or awakening is the extraordinary, sovereign work of God.

The role of the Church is not to produce revival but to prepare for it. John the Baptist was sent to prepare Israel to receive the work of God in Christ's first coming. Dr. Luke tells us, "This is the one about whom it is written, 'I will send my messenger ahead of you, who will prepare your way before you'" (Luke 7:27).

How does God prepare the Church? God "gave some to be apostles, some to be prophets, some to be evangelists, and some to be pastors and teachers, to prepare God's people for works of service, so that the body of Christ may be built up" (Ephesians 4:11-12).

What does it mean *"to prepare God's people"*? The same word Paul uses was also used by Matthew as he described the fishermen James and John "preparing their nets."[1] The preparation of the saints is similar to preparing fishing nets.

As the net had to be washed, so believers must be cleansed. As the net moved through the sea, it collected both good and bad (Matthew 13:47). The "bad" included unclean fish, seaweed, and debris. As we believers move about in this sin-cursed world, we are corrupted. Our effectiveness will always be in direct proportion to our personal holiness. To prepare for revival we must develop a sensitive conscience and keep short accounts with God (see 1 John 1:9).

As the net had to be dried in the light of the sun, so believers must spend time in fellowship with God's Son. The net would rot if it were not dried out after every use. Fishermen dried their nets by spreading them in the sun on bare rock (see Ezekiel 26:5, 14). Even though the nets were made to be used in the sea, if the sea's moisture remained in the nets, the strands would rot.

Believers must spend time in the presence of God's Son. Jesus "appointed twelve—designating them apostles—that they might be with him and that he might send them out to preach and to have authority to drive out demons" (Mark 3:14-15). Before the apostles could preach, have authority, or drive out demons, they had to spend time with Jesus Christ. The Jewish officials could tell that the apostles had been with Jesus (Acts 4:13). It takes time *with* the Lord to be able to do our work *for* the Lord (see John 15:1-8).

As the net had to be mended, so believers must be trained. Nets would sometimes break under the weight of the catch.[2] Also, the net would sometimes get torn or snagged. The broken strands would allow the good fish to swim through the holes. When this happened, the nets were not accomplishing what they were made for.

Believers moving through life experience wear and tear. Sometimes the stresses are seemingly more than can be borne. Spiritual battles leave Christians battered and beaten. This leaves us with large gaps in our lives. Our ability to minister for Christ suffers, and unbelievers we should win to the Savior swim right through the holes. To repair the torn places, believers must be trained to use the means of grace properly, the classical spiritual disciplines and godly examples. The means of grace are the word and prayer. Spiritual disciplines are "activities undertaken to bring us into more effective cooperation with Christ and his kingdom."[3] Scripture teaches that believers should be influenced by one another's good example.

Proper use of the means of grace, spiritual disciplines, and godly examples will renew us personally so that we grow in Christlike character. Renewed believers—especially officers—can then be used to revitalize their local churches. The revitalization of local churches is essential for the reformation of the Church.

This revitalization comes when the local church returns to being the missionary organism God intended her to be. Then worship provides joyful expectancy. The pastor prays fervently. The leadership team prays ardently on behalf of the congregation. The whole church engages in prayer as a world-class weapon in the battle against evil and cherishes prayer as a means of intimate and constant communication with God. Preaching and teaching is Bible-centered and powerful. Fellowship changes lives through reconciliation and sanctification. Discipline is Bible-based and consistently exercised. Outreach results in new converts regularly entering the life of the church. Ministry is pastor-led and lay-driven. Leaders and workers are multiplied through a committed core group, and, as needed and able, they minister in local churches other than their own. Their strategic plan is a written statement of vision and strategy for achieving that vision. The congregation is teachable. The people are open to hear what the leaders have to say and are willing to submit to God-appointed leadership. The congregation is a transforming counterculture. Financial resources are adequate. The facility is adequate but not extravagant.

Renewed believers and revitalized congregations, by God's grace, can fulfill the purpose for which they were originally made—to glorify God and enjoy Him forever! Renewed believers and revitalized congregations will be prepared for the coming Great Awakening!

It is essential that those who are concerned about revival and spiritual awakening maintain fellowship with each other. It is also important to avoid developing new structures and programs that cause unnecessary congestion in the church's already crowded calendar. Here is how you can do both.

Plan for regular monthly meetings in which you do three things. First, pray for revival and spiritual awakening.

Second, discuss significant material on the subjects of revival, awakening, personal renewal, and local church revitalization. This might include more of Jonathan Edwards's materials, such as his sermons:

- *The Most High a Prayer-Hearing God*—Psalm 65:2.
- *Hypocrites Deficient in the Duty of Prayer*—Job 27:10.
- *Christian Cautions in the Necessity of Self-Examination*— Psalm 139:23-24.
- *The Preciousness of Time and the Importance of Redeeming It*—Ephesians 5:16.

Third, report on what you are doing in the areas of renewal and revitalization.

Pastors should be the first leaders of Key Covenant Teams (KCTs). They should each recruit and train an assistant. After the first discussion of *The Spirit of Revival*, the assistant becomes the leader for a second KCT. He too selects an assistant, and when the second series of discussions is completed, participants from that team are urged to become a part of the ongoing Key Covenant Fellowship (KCF) in their local church. (This process is described and developed more fully later in this book—see pages 169-170.) This will provide a growing group of people who encourage each other to pray for awakening and work for personal renewal and church revitalization. In this way God will prepare us for His mighty work of revival and awakening!

FOOTNOTES TO THIS SECTION

1. "Going on from there, he saw two other brothers, James son of Zebedee and his brother John. They were in a boat with their father Zebedee, preparing their nets. Jesus called them" (Matthew 4:21).

2. See John 21:6.

3. Dallas Willard, *The Spirit of the Disciplines* (New York: Harper & Row, 1988), p. 156.

APPENDIX

Watch for Revival

> *"No one knows about that day or hour, not even the angels in heaven, nor the Son, but only the Father. Be on guard! Be alert! You do not know when that time will come. It's like a man going away: He leaves his house in charge of his servants, each with his assigned task, and tells the one at the door to keep watch. Therefore keep watch because you do not know when the owner of the house will come back—whether in the evening, or at midnight, or when the rooster crows, or at dawn. If he comes suddenly, do not let him find you sleeping. What I say to you, I say to everyone: 'Watch!'"*
>
> —Mark 13:32-37

Soldier of Christ, you are in an enemy's country. Keep watch as the Lord instructed.

What does it mean to watch? My first night in navy boot camp was memorable. From lights out to reveille I heard the clopping sound of combat boots marching up and down the barracks. At roll call the next morning our drill instructor asked, "Men, how did you sleep last night?"

Without thinking, I blurted out, "Nobody could sleep last night. Somebody was walking up and down in the barracks all night long."

The chief fiendishly grinned at me and said, "Parrish, you won't be bothered by someone else's footsteps tonight. You've got the watch from midnight to 4 A.M." Then he warned us, "Standing watch is one of the most important things you'll ever learn. Never leave your watch until you are properly relieved. If you are ever caught sleeping or drinking on watch, you will be court-martialed. Someday your life and the lives of your buddies may depend on the way you stand your watch. Stay awake! Stay alert! Stay alive!"

This was my introduction to standing watch. We had 120 men in Easy Company. Every hour of the day and night two men were standing watch—one inside the barracks and one outside. When I was assigned to the Marines, we went on field exercises. Sometimes we practiced having half the men watching while the other half slept. I never complained again, though it all seemed unnecessary and a little stupid—until I found myself in combat in Korea!

During the siege of Hagaru, nobody slept. I went forty hours without closing my eyes. When the temperature hovered between 25 and 30 degrees below zero, everyone, including the Chinese, functioned at only about half their usual effectiveness, and watching was very difficult.

We cannot watch without staying awake, but staying awake is not enough. If you don't know what you are looking for, you will not recognize it when you see it. Knowing what to look for puts the mind in an expectant search mode.

As a medical corpsman in a combat zone, my primary job was not to kill the enemy. However, I did have to constantly watch for the enemy or he would kill me. My job was to keep wounded Marines alive so they could kill the enemy. The wounded were in two groups—those who could still fight and those who could no longer fight. An airstrip had been constructed in Hagaru so we could fly the seriously wounded out of harm's way. Some men had serious wounds, yet wanted to stay with their buddies. Other men had superficial wounds but wanted to get out of combat. We needed all the men who could still fight to increase our ability to get the division out, but all who stayed ran a high risk of not going home alive.

The wounded who could no longer fight were also in two groups—those who could be helped and those who were beyond help. Among those who could be helped, I had to determine who could have morphine for their pain and who could not. Morphine would kill a man with a head wound. The morphine came in Syrettes, tubes topped with a sterile needle enclosed in a plastic cover. It was so cold I had to defrost the Syrettes by placing them in my mouth, one inside each cheek. I had to watch the state of the wounded we had in the tents. Some were killed by sniper fire while they lay on stretchers waiting to be evacuated.

In most cases the decision that someone was beyond medical help meant the man would soon die. It has been more than forty years and yet I can still vividly see those dying men—for example, the eighteen-year-old Marine with the top of his head torn away by mortar fragments. All I could do was tie him between two stretchers so he wouldn't wander around and interfere with treatment of the men we could save. Every time I passed him, he was talking about his wife and child. In about an hour he was dead.

Watching, staying awake, staying alert for all these things and many more, was absolutely essential to staying alive, surviving the battle, and one day returning home.

As in the military, so it is with the spiritual life. This world is enemy territory. God tells us, "Do not love the world or anything in the world. If anyone loves the world, the love of the Father is not in him. For everything in the world—the cravings of sinful man, the lust of his eyes and the boasting of what he has and does—comes not from the Father but from the world. The world and its desires pass away, but the man who does the will of God lives forever" (1 John 2:15-17).

Jesus declared, "What I say to you, I say to everyone: 'Watch!'" (Mark 13:37). In classic Christian teaching, spiritual warfare is seen primarily as the believer's struggle with the flesh, the devil, and the world, for the purpose of one's own sanctification.[1] Each Christian is normally responsible for himself or herself. Paul strikes the balance between individual responsibility and group interdependence. To the group he says, " Carry each other's burdens, and in this way you will fulfill the law of Christ" (Galatians 6:2). Then he tells individuals, "each one should carry his own load" (verse 5). The key to understanding Paul's teaching is to note the difference between "burdens" and "load." When the individual has reached his or her limit of what can be carried alone ("load"), the group is to come alongside and help with the "burden," that which the individual cannot carry. Burdens can relate to the weight of a thing—it may simply be too heavy—or the nature of the thing—the individual's wisdom or abilities are not sufficient to deal with the situation.

In addition to burden-bearing, Scripture teaches that fathers have special responsibility for their families, and pastors bear responsibility for their flocks. To the elders of the Ephesian church Paul commanded, "Guard yourselves and all the flock of which the Holy Spirit has made you overseers. Be shepherds of the church of God, which he bought with his own blood. I know that after I leave, savage wolves will come in among you and will not spare the flock. Even from your own number men will arise and distort the truth in order to draw away disciples after them. So be on your guard! Remember that for three years I never stopped warning each of you night and day with tears" (Acts 20:28-31).

The psalmist reminds us, "He will not let your foot slip—he who watches over you will not slumber; indeed, he who watches over Israel will neither slumber nor sleep" (Psalm 121:3-4). An implication in these words is that God is the only One who does not need sleep. No one can stay on watch twenty-four hours a day, day after day after day. We must work together.

Stay Awake!

The first step in staying awake is to be sure we are converted. Saint Augustine tells of his conversion. He was in a garden and heard a voice say, "Take and read." There on a bench was a portion of Scripture. He picked it up and read Romans 13:11-14.

> *And do this, understanding the present time. The hour has come for you to wake up from your slumber, because our salvation is nearer now than when we first believed. The night is nearly over; the day is almost here. So let us put aside the deeds of darkness and put on the armor of light. Let us behave decently, as in the daytime, not in orgies and drunkenness, not in sexual immorality and debauchery, not in dissension and jealousy. Rather, clothe*

*yourselves with the Lord Jesus Christ, and do not think
about how to gratify the desires of the sinful nature.*

God awoke Augustine from his deadly sleep of sin, and he surrendered to Christ for his salvation. Has God awakened you?
Have you surrendered to the Savior? If not, do so now.

The second step in staying awake is to be a person of light
in the midst of the night. "You, brothers, are not in darkness so
that this day should surprise you like a thief. You are all sons of
the light and sons of the day. We do not belong to the night or
to the darkness. So then, let us not be like others, who are asleep,
but let us be alert and self-controlled. For those who sleep, sleep
at night, and those who get drunk, get drunk at night. But since
we belong to the day, let us be self-controlled, putting on faith
and love as a breastplate, and the hope of salvation as a helmet"
(1 Thessalonians 5:4-8).

Stay Alert!

We are to stay "alert" and "self-controlled" (see 1 Thessalonians
5:6, 8; cf. Colossians 4:2). We are to remember what we have
received and heard and hold it fast; we are to repent (Revelation
3:2-3). We must watch to see that the *ordinary* means of grace
are properly used in our churches. And we must watch to see
that the alleged *extraordinary* manifestations of grace are according to the word of God.

The climax of all history will be the return of Christ to this
earth. Revival is but a small foretaste of our Lord's Second
Coming. When His bride is complete, He will claim her for His

own. Thus we are to watch for the *parousia*, the coming of the Lord. We are to expect His appearing at any moment (1 Thessalonians 5:2, 6). "Look, he is coming with the clouds, and every eye will see him, even those who pierced him; and all the peoples of the earth will mourn because of him. So shall it be! Amen" (Revelation 1:7). By the power of the Spirit of truth we are to watch for that which exalts Jesus, attacks Satan's interests, exalts the Holy Scriptures, lifts up sound doctrine, and promotes love for God and man (see 1 John 4:1-21).

> **By the power of the Spirit of truth we are to watch for that which exalts Jesus, attacks Satan's interests, exalts the Holy Scriptures, lifts up sound doctrine, and promotes love for God and man.**

In the meantime we are to watch for the enemies of the soul—the world, the flesh, and the devil. Peter commands, "Be *self-controlled* and *alert*. Your enemy the devil prowls around like a roaring lion looking for someone to devour" (1 Peter 5:8). Satan seeks to destroy through false prophets who come in sheep's clothing but inwardly are ferocious wolves (Matthew 7:15). Therefore, Jesus tells us to watch so that no one deceives us (Matthew 24:4). As the accuser of the brothers, Satan will try to cause divisions and put up obstacles. Paul urges us to "watch out for those who cause divisions and put obstacles in your way that are contrary to the teaching you have learned. Keep away from them" (Romans 16:17).

The flesh is the most strategic foe. The world and the devil cannot defeat us if the flesh does not allow it. The flesh encourages dead orthodoxy and spiritual pride. The world tries to negate the power of the Spirit with humanistic compromises of biblical truth. So Jesus warns us, "Watch out for the teachers of the law. They like to walk around in flowing robes and be greeted in the marketplaces" (Mark 12:38). "Watch out for the yeast of the Pharisees [legalism] and that of Herod [secularism]" (Mark 8:15). The flesh craves material things (materialism); so Jesus tells us, "Watch out! Be on your guard against all kinds of greed; a man's life does not consist in the abundance of his possessions" (Luke 12:15).

We stay alert by strengthening "what remains and is about to die" (Revelation 3:2). We stay alert by recognizing the willingness of the spirit and the weakness of the flesh and praying that we will not enter into temptation (Mark 14:38; cf. Matthew 26:41). Watching and praying to avoid temptation is hard work. Jesus warns, "Be careful, or your hearts will be weighed down with dissipation, drunkenness and the anxieties of life, and that day will close on you unexpectedly like a trap" (Luke 21:34). When Jesus found Peter, James, and John sleeping, He said, "Could you men not keep watch with me for one hour?" (Matthew 26:40b). This prayer is to be "in the Spirit on all occasions with all kinds of prayers and requests. With this in mind, be alert and always keep on praying for all the saints" (Ephesians 6:18).

Watching for revival does not mean passively waiting. Jesus told his servants to "occupy" until he comes (Luke 19:13, KJV). Pastors should preach on texts that describe God's extraordinary work of revival. Two helpful volumes for preachers are *Salvation in Full Color—Twenty Sermons by Great Awakening Preachers* and *Sanctify the Congregation—Preparing the*

Church for a Solemn Assembly. Both of these works are edited by Richard Owen Roberts and may be obtained from International Awakening Press, P.O. Box 232, Wheaton, IL 60189-0232. Another fine volume is John Piper's *God's Passion for His Glory*, a thoughtful treatise on another of Jonathan Edwards's major works.

Stay Alive!

Watching results in a life that is blessed by Christ. Jesus pronounces, "Blessed is he who stays awake and keeps his clothes with him, so that he may not go naked and be shamefully exposed" (Revelation 16:15). Church leaders should encourage their members to band together in small groups to watch for revival by prayer, fasting, repentance, seeking after God's face, mutual encouragement, and study of God's word and classic writings on revival. One approach to such "banding" is Key Covenant Teams (KCT).

What Is a Key Covenant Team?

Key Covenant Teams (KCTs) are like guerrilla fighters on a special mission. They are Christians who band together because they believe wholeheartedly in the concepts expressed in the Key Covenant (see below).

A KCT should have no less than four and no more than twelve participants. The dynamic for discipleship is diminished with fewer than four people; with more than twelve, individuals can get lost in the crowd. Members of a KCT commit themselves to God and one another for a specific mission to be accomplished in a specific period of time.

Members of KCTs watch for revival as they work by grace through faith for more vital churches. Churches become more vital as individual believers increase their own personal spirituality. Personal spirituality consists of the dominion of the Spirit in an individual's life. This can be increased by proper use of the spiritual disciplines. As noted before, spiritual disciplines are "activities undertaken to bring us into more effective cooperation with Christ and his kingdom."[2]

Personal spirituality consists of the dominion of the Spirit in an individual's life.

The Lord Jesus provides the model for the KCT band. He spent most of His time with the Twelve (Matthew 10:1; 11:1; 20:17; 26:20; Mark 3:14; 4:10; 6:7; 9:35; 10:32; Luke 6:13; 8:1; 9:1; 18:31; etc.). Among the Twelve, three formed an inner circle who were with Him at the most critical times (Matthew 17:1; Mark 5:37; 13:3; 14:33). KCTs consist of Christians who commit themselves to God and one another to do God's will in this world.

Pastors should usually be the first leaders of the KCTs in their local churches. KCTs can be ongoing catalysts for personal and corporate spirituality if the pastor/leader plans from the beginning to complete the following three stages:

Stage One: Pastor-Leader Preparation. The pastor begins with prayer for guidance. He takes about six weeks to read *The Spirit of Revival*, including the Discussion Guide and the Leader's Guide (the latter is available from Serve International). This gives him familiarity with the material so that he is more comfortable starting the KCTs. Then the pastor recruits a lay leader to be his assistant, and together they recruit another four to twelve participants. This first group should include official leaders of the church.

Stage Two: Launch the First KCT Group. This consists of six sessions, usually one a week for six weeks. The agendas for each of these sessions is contained in the Leader's Guide (available from Serve International).

Stage Three: Reproducing KCTs and Developing Ongoing Key Covenant Fellowships (KCFs). This stage consists of two tracks. Track One is the birth of additional KCTs. The assistant for the first team becomes the leader of a second team. He recruits an assistant from the first team, and together they recruit four to twelve new participants and conduct another KCT. This process of the assistant becoming the leader and recruiting an assistant from a KCT that has completed Stage Two is repeated after each series of discussions is completed; participants are urged to become a part of the Track Two ongoing KCF in their local church.

Track Two is an ongoing monthly KCF for all participants who have completed the discussion of *The Spirit of Revival*. Each person in the ongoing KCF pairs up with one other participant. They pray together once a week. They encourage each other to pray, to study revival, to work for their own spiritual growth, and to work with their pastors for increased church vitality. Once a month, under the pastor's leadership, they meet with the ongoing KCF. This monthly meeting provides opportunity for mutual encouragement, prayer for revival, and discussion of selected materials.

The pastor leads regular monthly meetings in which participants do three things. First, they pray for revival and spiritual awakening. Second, they read, journal, and discuss significant material on the subjects of revival and personal and corporate spirituality. This material may include sermons of Jonathan Edwards. Third, they report on what they are doing in the areas of personal and corporate spirituality.

Lay leaders who continually recruit and lead discussions of *The Spirit of Revival* will provide the potential for growing numbers of people to participate in ongoing KCFs.

We will now examine the Key Covenant, so crucial to all that we are seeking to inspire and equip in this book.

The Key Covenant

This covenant is as follows:

I believe a balanced blend of belief and behavior produces godliness. Belief without behavior is dead orthodoxy. Behavior without belief is hypocrisy. The Key Covenant seeks this balance of belief and behavior. In the statements below, beliefs are printed in normal type; behaviors are printed in bold type.

I believe praying for revival in the church, awakening in the culture, and working by grace through faith for my personal renewal and the revitalization of my local church are keys to preparing for God's extraordinary work. *I covenant* with God and the members of the Key Covenant Team that, guided by the precepts summarized under the acrostic TEAMS, I will watch for revival and work to make my local church more vital.

TRUTH

I believe truth is ultimate reality that can be known only through the person of the Lord Jesus Christ. He is the living Word revealed in the written word, the inerrant, inspired Scripture (John 14:6; 17:17). *I believe* the Spirit of truth always exalts Jesus, attacks Satan's interests, exalts the Holy Scriptures, lifts up sound doctrine, and promotes love for God and man. *I believe* my Christian life must be built on the objective truth of God's Word and that all subjective experience must be evaluated by this objective truth. *I believe* this word is the weapon by which, in the power of the Holy Spirit, my life mission will be accomplished (Ephesians 6:17; 2 Timothy 3:16-17; Hebrews 4:12).

Therefore, I will watch my life and doctrine closely. I will carefully study the Scriptures, faithfully practice what I learn, and regularly proclaim God's truth!

EQUIPPING

I believe equipping is achieved through proper use of the means of grace, spiritual disciplines, and godly examples. *I believe* equipping is not passive learning but active development of essential ministry competencies. *I believe* equipping produces not merely students with head knowledge but godly, fruitful disciples who use their spiritual gifts to equip others (Ephesians 4:12; 2 Timothy 2:2; James 1:22-25).

Therefore, I commit myself to the lifelong process of being equipped and equipping others!

ACCOUNTABILITY

I believe voluntary submission of myself to a small group of Christians will help me grow more like Jesus Christ. These groups should not be composed of people who are all on the same level of spiritual maturity. Each group should have a leader. Each member of the group must be willing to encourage the others to judge themselves properly, to persevere in personal holiness, and to attempt significant ministry for the Lord (1 Corinthians 11:31; Ephesians 5:21; James 5:16).

Therefore, I will periodically examine myself, participate regularly in a Key Covenant Team, and submit myself to a member of this team.

MISSION

I believe my life mission is to "make disciples" as stated in the Great Commission. *I believe* this mission must be energized by Great-Commandment love—loving the Lord with all my being, loving my neighbors as myself. *I believe* I am to make disciples by going forth with the Gospel. *I believe* I am to encourage new believers to be baptized into vital local churches and to learn all that Jesus commanded them. *I believe* my mission begins with my family (Matthew 28:18-20; John 17:17-18; 2 Corinthians 5:18, 20). *I believe* Great-Commandment love produces reconciliation between believers of both genders and in all races and cultures.

Therefore, I expect the Holy Spirit to use me often to proclaim the Gospel and win others to faith in Christ and encourage them to pursue vital membership in local churches; and I commit myself to be a bridge-builder to Christians of other races.

SUPPLICATION

I believe supplication is communication and communion that increases my intimacy with and my commitment to God. *I believe* prayer should focus on hastening the coming of the kingdom of God. As the Holy Spirit enables me to pray, I become God's coworker, achieving His will in this world. *I believe* prayer conditions me to receive the answers God gives and provides the power to wield the weapon of the word to fulfill my mission. *I believe* Kingdom-focused prayer requires significant private daily time. *I believe* the spiritual disciplines of solitude, silence, meditation, journaling, and obedient action empower prayer. *I believe* I must focus my prayer on my family and the laborers and leadership of my local church, especially my pastor. *I believe* that when I properly use the spiritual discipline of fasting, it helps me develop a more spiritual perception of life and can be used by God to break the culture's materialistic, hedonistic hold on my life. *I believe* extraordinary prayer with fasting will achieve extraordinary results (Luke 18:1; Ephesians 6:18; Philippians 4:6; James 5:16).

Therefore, I will spend significant time daily in private prayer, I will pray with a kingdom focus for my family and my church leaders and laborers, and I will spend one day each quarter in extraordinary fasting and prayer for personal renewal, local church revitalization, revival, and awakening.

Signature: _____ Date: _____

Church _____

Address _____

City State Zip _____

Making the Key Covenant Personally Relevant

The twenty-three questions below will help you examine your life by the statements in the Covenant. Determine the key points that you believe God wants you to improve through another Key Covenant Team member's encouragement. As relationships in your team develop, you will be able to work on deeper issues. It is very important that team members not be forced to deal with things that push them too far too fast.

TRUTH

1. How much time do I spend in personal Bible study? Is this adequate time?

2. How do I practice what I learn from my Bible study?

3. With whom do I share regularly what I learn?

EQUIPPING

4. How am I being equipped?

5. How am I equipping someone else?

ACCOUNTABILITY

6. How well do I "judge" myself in matters of truth and personal holiness?

7. How do I properly guard my relations with members of the opposite sex?

8. How do I guard myself against the suggestive and explicit sexual material so prevalent in our culture?

9. How do I keep integrity in all my financial dealings?

10. How well am I doing in giving priority time to my family?

11. How well am I fulfilling the mandates of my calling (redemptive and cultural)?

MISSION

12. What initiative am I taking to promote reconciliation between believers of all races, cultures, and different denominations?

13. How effective am I in making disciples of all nations?

14. How effective am I in making disciples of the members of my family?

15. How consistent am I in proclaiming the Gospel?

16. How consistent am I in winning others to Christ?

SUPPLICATION

17. How much time do I spend in individual daily prayer? Is this adequate time?

18. Do I pray regularly with and for my family?

19. Do I pray regularly with and for my local church family?

20. Do I pray regularly that the leadership of my local church will exemplify the character standards set forth in Scripture?

21. Do I pray regularly for my pastor each time I have grace at meals?

22. Do I spend one day each quarter in special prayer and fasting?

23. What are the items the Lord wants me to ask someone else to encourage me to improve?

FOOTNOTES TO THIS SECTION

1. See Bryan Zacharias, *The Embattled Christian* (Carlisle, Penn.: Banner of Truth, n.d.).
2. Dallas Willard, *The Spirit of the Disciplines* (New York: Harper & Row, 1988), p. 156.

DISCUSSION GUIDE

Getting the Most Out of a Key Covenant Team

Throughout history, when the church has found itself in moral and spiritual decay, God's people have banded together in prayer, fasting, repentance, and in seeking after His face. Time after time God has come among His returning people in profound power, reviving His church. (Richard Owen Roberts)

Six activities will help you personally become more spiritually vital and thus better prepared for revival and reformation. *Praying* will make you a focused person. *Reading* will make you an informed person. *Writing* will make you an exact person. *Meeting* will make you a bonded person. *Discussing* will make you an insightful person. *Doing* will make you a growing person.

PRAYING WILL MAKE YOU A FOCUSED PERSON

Prayerful study focuses your mind on discovering God's will. At the beginning of each session you will find the following printed prayer: "Lord, revive me and revive my Key Covenant Teammates. Revive my church and my pastor. Lord, give me helpful insights and understanding from what I am about to study. Show me what I need to understand better. As You show me things I am eager to try, enable me to do them. As You show me things that I find hard to apply to my life, help me be honest about them.

Lord, as I review the questions in the Discussion Guide, focus my mind and help me find the truth in what I study." Pray this prayer aloud each time before you study.

As you study the assigned material, frequently pause and ask the Holy Spirit to give you understanding. Anytime you find your mind wandering, ask the Lord to refocus your mind.

READING WILL MAKE YOU AN INFORMED PERSON

As a member of a Key Covenant Team you agree to read selected material according to a specific schedule.

Start by rapidly reading the assigned material. Then read the section and write in your journal the answers to as many of the questions as time permits. Be sure to budget time to write your answers to the filter questions.

A Word About the Footnotes: The footnotes contain Bible verses that support statements in the text; this makes them readily available. Some footnotes also contain definitions and indicate other sources on the subject. So you will certainly find it profitable to examine the relevant notes for the whole book as you work your way through the Discussion Guide.

Three Guards: Your mind will be at work as you read. But before you own anything in your heart, it must pass through three guards that protect your heart. Each guard is an automatic reaction; you may be unaware of it, and yet you experience it. The three guards are as follows:

1. *The Guard of Understanding.* You must understand something in order to respond properly.

2. *The Ethical Guard* (what you believe to be right and wrong). After you understand something, it is more likely that you

will do it if you believe it is right. You cannot do what you believe to be wrong without violating your conscience.

God's Word is *always* right, but some of its teachings may be hard for you to apply. When you find a hard saying, don't just pass over it. Make note of it. Pray that God will help you properly respond. Share your concern with your Christian friends in a Key Covenant Team, and ask them to help you.

3. *The Emotional Guard* is your concern for your own well-being. If you understand something and believe it is right but fear that doing it will hurt you more than help you, you will struggle with doing it or may not even try to do it. At times you will need to weigh apparent present benefits against actual eternal benefits. Paul put it this way: "I consider that our present sufferings are not worth comparing with the glory that will be revealed in us" (Romans 8:18).

Four Filter Questions. Four questions will help you deal with your three guards. Tuck these away in your mind:

1. What helpful insights do I understand from this section? (understanding)

2. What do I want to understand better? (understanding)

3. What is God telling me to do that I'm not afraid to try? (emotional)

4. What is God telling me that I find hard to apply to my life? (ethical or emotional)

The Bible says, "Seek and you will find" (Matthew 7:7). Review the four filter questions before you begin to read each chapter. These questions engage your mind to search for truth. At the end of each section, react to your thoughts in the light of these questions. Write your thinking in your journal.

As you read, it may be helpful to do the following:

1. Look for things that you understand and are eager to do. Place a star ★ beside these.

2. Put a question mark ? beside anything you do not understand.

3. Note anything that threatens you with an **X**. Also indicate why it threatens you.

Anytime you try to be what the Lord desires, the devil makes sure at some point that you feel threatened. Deal with the things that frighten you. "For God has not given us a spirit of fear, but of power and of love and of a sound mind" (2 Timothy 1:7, NKJV). Face fear with "a sound mind" (self-discipline) and it will vanish.

Writing Will Make You an Exact Person

All members of the group should keep a personal journal in which they write answers to the filter questions and their responses to the Discussion Guide questions as time permits.

Obviously, the more you put into this study, the more you will receive from it. However, do not let the thought of writing your answers to the questions in your journal overwhelm you. Try this: invest at least thirty minutes a day, five days per week for each assignment. That may sound like a lot, but it is really very workable.

If you are not involved in a Key Covenant Team, remember that you will receive most from this effort if you regularly discuss this material with other believers. This will be challenging, but it should not be overwhelming.

Personal Journal. Life that is worth living is worth recording. It is impossible to overestimate the increased benefit you will gain from each assignment if you write your response to the four filter questions and the questions in the Discussion Guide. When you are in a Key Covenant Team, sharing these written thoughts will bless both you and others on the team.

Here are some practical suggestions for journal keeping:

• Whatever works for you, do it. Make this as convenient as possible. You can carry a small, blank notebook in your coat pocket or purse. Or you may find it helpful to use a larger notebook.

• If you write your journal in longhand, be sure to write enough to retain your full thought. If you are able to use a word processor and one is convenient for you, try it.

• Don't worry about sentence structure, spelling, or penmanship. You will be the only one seeing your writing.

• Don't just copy words from the text. Throughout the Discussion Guide, you will see the questions, "Do you agree? Why?" It is important to think all this through. Don't blindly accept the thoughts in the text.

When you join a Team, the first thing you should do is write the Key Covenant in your journal. Before a man was crowned king over Israel, he was required to write the law of the covenant in his own hand. This reinforced his knowledge of his responsibilities under the covenant. This handwritten copy of the law was evidence that he willingly assumed the covenant's responsibilities.[1] Let journal keeping become a life-long habit, and you will find new depth in your relationship with Jesus.

MEETING WILL MAKE YOU A BONDED PERSON

The Key Covenant Team will meet as a group at the time and place agreed upon. The meeting place should be free from unnecessary distractions. It should be a place where you can easily talk to each other and pray together.

Each Key Covenant Team member pairs up with one other person as a prayer partner. They pray for each other daily. They sit together during the group discussion and dialogue with another pair of prayer partners. If one is absent from the team meeting, his or her partner should make contact to see that the partner stays current on the matters of the Key Covenant Team. Prayer partners provide the deepest level of encouragement. As they grow closer to one another, they ask to be encouraged for more and more significant matters in their lives.

DISCUSSING WILL MAKE YOU AN INSIGHTFUL PERSON

In the meeting the members discuss their responses. It is impossible to discuss all the questions provided in the Guide in each session. Specific questions will be dealt with, but most of the discussion time will be focused on responses to the filter questions. The discussion should take about one hour.

If the group is larger than six, at points in the discussion you will be asked to form into groups of three or four and interact with each other. Be prepared to express your thinking in these small groups.

After you discuss in the smaller groups, there will be time for discussion in the whole group. In this way you will receive maximum benefit from this group.

Doing Will Make You a Growing Person

The apostle James exhorts:

> *Do not merely listen to the word, and so deceive your-*
> *selves. Do what it says. Anyone who listens to the word*
> *but does not do what it says is like a man who looks at*
> *his face in a mirror and, after looking at himself, goes*
> *away and immediately forgets what he looks like. But*
> *the man who looks intently into the perfect law that*
> *gives freedom, and continues to do this, not forgetting*
> *what he has heard, but doing it—he will be blessed in*
> *what he does.*
>
> —James 1:22-25

An old maxim says, "Knowledge is power." The words of James make it clear that knowledge without proper action is not power. Rather, it brings judgment! Therefore, each team member must seek to do what he or she believes the Lord is directing. Specific action steps should be shared with the group. Before the close of each meeting, time should be spent praying for one another. At the beginning of each session, there should be a brief time of reporting on progress in these actions.

Insight will come to those who pray and read. Greater understanding will come to those who, in addition to prayer and reading, record their responses to the four filter questions and the exercises in the Discussion Guide in a personal journal and then regularly meet to discuss this with other Christians. But ultimate benefit will come only to those who add obedience to all these steps and do God's will as He reveals it through this process.

People should sign the following commitment as a reminder of their assumption of their responsibilities to God and the other members of the Key Covenant Team.

Key Covenant Team
Commitment

I desire to be more spiritually vital and to help prepare my church for God-sent revival and reformation. To this end I covenant with the Lord and members of my team to meet _____ times (insert dates and times). God helping me, I will pray for the personal renewal of my team members and myself. I will read the selected materials as scheduled. I will write my responses to the filter questions and as many of the discussion questions as time allows. I will meet with the other members of my team at _____ (insert location) to discuss this material, and I will do what God shows me to prepare for revival and reformation.

_____
Signature

As a result of praying, reading, writing, meeting, discussing, and doing what God encourages me to do in this introduction to the study, I will be able to:

1. Explain the difference between revival and reformation, as these terms are used by R. C. Sproul.

2. Explain the six activities that will help me personally become more spiritually vital and thus better prepared for revival and reformation.

3. Explain the Key Covenant as summarized in the TEAMS acrostic.

4. Identify at least one area of my life I am willing to share with my prayer partner so he/she can encourage me to grow more like Christ in this area.

Pray this prayer aloud each time you study:

Lord, revive my soul and revive the souls of my Key Covenant Teammates. Revive my church and my pastor. Lord, give me helpful insights and understanding from what I am about to study. Show me what I need to understand better. As You show me things I am eager to try, enable me to do them. As You show me things that I find hard to apply to my life, help me be honest about them. Lord, as I review the questions in the Discussion Guide, focus my mind and help me find the truth in what I study.

Read the following:

• Read the four filter questions (page 179) to put your mind in a search mode.

• Review the Discussion Guide, pages 177-185.

• Read the Foreword by Archie Parrish and Introduction by R. C. Sproul, pages 11-39.

• Read the Appendix, pages 159-176.

Getting the Most out of a Key Covenant Team

Write the answers to the following questions in your journal:

1. In your own words describe a Key Covenant Team.

2. Explain in your own words the six activities necessary for participating in a Key Covenant.

3. Explain in your own words what the three guards are and how they function.

4. When should you review the four filter questions? Why?

5. The questions and responses to the Discussion Guide help you do what?

6. What do the footnotes contain?

7. Life that is worth living is worth _____.

Key Covenant Team Commitment

8. Explain in your own words why you are willing to sign the Key Covenant Team Commitment.

9. Explain in your own words the TEAMS acrostic of the Key Covenant.

10. Following the Key Covenant is a list of twenty-three questions to help you make the Key Covenant personally relevant.

Carefully read this covenant; then prayerfully examine your life using the questions. Ask the Lord to impress on you one area in your spiritual development to share with your small group in the KCT next week. They will encourage you and pray for you.

Archie Parrish's Introduction

11. What does Parrish say is the purpose of this edited work?

Sproul's Historical Introduction

12. Sproul asks, "What is the difference between *revival* and *reformation*?" How does he answer this question? Do you agree? Why?

13. What is the cultural context we must keep in view when we speak of spiritual revival and/or reformation?

14. Sproul says, "Significant events were unfolding within the church" during the cultural revolution of the sixties. What were these?

15. Sproul says that Edwards's *Distinguishing Marks* provides a map to follow for all such periods of revival and for that reason is of abiding value for us today. Why did he say this? Do you agree? Why?

16. "Edwards noted a difference between faith and credulity. Credulity is faith without substance, an easy-believism that lacks critical judgment and consequently discernment." What is the significance of this in relation to revival?

17. List the negative signs.

18. List the positive signs.

"Very often some text of Scripture expressing God's sovereignty has been impressed upon their minds. By this they have been calmed. They have been brought, as it were, to lie at God's feet. And after great agonies they have been composed and quiet in submission to a just and sovereign God" (Jonathan Edwards).

Write the following Scripture verse on a card and carry it with you. Read it aloud to yourself many times daily. Use it in your prayers.

"You are worthy, our Lord and God, to receive glory and honor and power, for you created all things, and by your will they were created and have their being" (Revelation 4:11).

Write your response to the material for this session in light of the four filter questions on page 179.

Write your evaluation of this session after the discussion. Evaluation forms are provided in the Leader's Guide.

SESSION TWO

As a result of praying, reading, writing, meeting, discussing, and doing what God encourages me to do from this introduction to the study, I will be able to:

1. Explain Edwards's design in writing his book.

2. Explain the Holy Spirit's extraordinary influences and gifts, and His ordinary operations.

3. Explain the devil's mimicking of the work of the Holy Spirit.

4. Optional: Examine my own spiritual condition before the Lord.

Pray this prayer aloud each time you study.

Lord, revive my soul and revive the souls of my Key Covenant Teammates. Revive my church and my pastor. Lord, give me helpful insights and understanding from what I am about to study. Show me what I need to understand better. As You show me things I am eager to try, enable me to do them. As You show me things that I find hard to apply to my life, help me be honest about them. Lord, as I review the questions in the Discussion Guide, focus my mind and help me find the truth in what I study.

Read the following.

• If you still need help in the procedure to get the most from your KCT, review the Discussion Guide, pages 177-185.

• Scan the four filter questions (page 179) to put your mind in a search mode.

• Read *Preface* by William Cooper, pages 43-51 and *The Spirit of Revival,* pages 53-55.

• At least once, read aloud the Key Covenant, pages 170-173.

William Cooper's Preface

Write the answers to the following questions in your journal.

1. What was the state of the church at the time of the Reformation?

2. What was the state of the church at the time Cooper wrote?

3. How does Cooper's description of his day compare with today?

4. Describe the extraordinary pouring out of the Spirit at the time Cooper wrote. What would such an outpouring look like in today's culture?

The Distinguishing Marks of a Work of the Spirit of God by Jonathan Edwards

5. Write in your journal your explanation of the Holy Spirit's extraordinary influences and gifts, and His ordinary operations.

6. Write in your journal your explanation of the devil's mimicking of the work of the Holy Spirit.

7. What was Edwards's design in writing this book?

8. What role does Scripture have in distinguishing the work of the Holy Spirit?

"Very often some text of Scripture expressing God's sovereignty has been impressed upon their minds. By this they have been calmed. They have been brought, as it were, to lie at God's feet. And after great agonies they have been composed and quiet in submission to a just and sovereign God" (Jonathan Edwards).

Write the following Scripture verse on a card and carry it with you. Read it aloud to yourself many times daily. Use it in your prayers.

"Dear friends, do not believe every spirit, but test the spirits to see whether they are from God, because many false prophets have gone out into the world" (1 John 4:1).

Write your response to the material for this session in light of the four filter questions on page 179.

Write your evaluation of this session after the discussion on the form provided by your leader.

SESSION THREE

As a result of praying, reading, writing, meeting, discussing, and doing what God encourages me to do from "Indifferent Signs," I will be able to:

1. Define an indifferent sign.

2. List the nine indifferent signs according to Edwards.

3. Explain each of these indifferent signs to another Christian.

Pray this prayer aloud each time you study.

Lord, revive my soul and revive the souls of my Key Covenant Teammates. Revive my church and my pastor. Lord, give me helpful insights and understanding from what I am about to study. Show me what I need to understand better. As You show me things I am eager to try, enable me to do them. As You show me things that I find hard to apply to my life, help me be honest about them. Lord, as I review the questions in the Discussion Guide, focus my mind and help me find the truth in what I study.

Write in your journal Edwards's nine indifferent signs.

Review the Table of Contents to see how the "Indifferent Signs" fit with the whole.

Read the following:

• If you still need help preparing for the KCT meeting, review again the Discussion Guide, pages 177-185.

• Scan the four filter questions (page 179) to put your mind in a search mode.

- Read *The Spirit of Revival*, "Indifferent Signs," pages 57-86.
- At least once, read aloud the Key Covenant, pages 170-173.

Section I: Indifferent Signs: Elements That Are Neither Sure Signs of the Spirit Nor Marks of the Flesh or the Devil

Write the answers to the following questions in your journal.

I. IT IS CARRIED ON IN AN UNUSUAL AND EXTRAORDINARY WAY

1. What does it mean to say that a work is carried on in an unusual and extraordinary way?

2. The variety of differences must still be understood within the limits of _____ rules.

3. What are some examples of how God has previously acted in an obviously unusual manner?

4. Edwards says, "We ought not to limit God where He has not limited Himself." What are some ways Christians limit God where He does not limit Himself?

5. "There is a great ability in persons to doubt strange things." Is this true of you?

II. INVOLUNTARY BODILY MOVEMENT MAY OCCUR

6. What were some of the physical reactions Edwards mentioned?

7. How does Edwards account for physical reactions?

III. IT PRODUCES MUCH TALK ABOUT THE CHRISTIAN FAITH

8. Do you agree with Edwards about this? Why?

9. When God's Spirit moves in our day, what "noise" should we expect from religious leaders and the secular media?

IV. Intense Religious Emotions Are Present

10. What great impressions did Edwards say were made on people's emotions?

11. How does Edwards explain these great impressions?

V. Example Is a Great Means

12. Explain how example is a great means of the Spirit's works.

13. What do you think of Edwards's explanation of God's use of example?

14. How does example relate to the proclamation of the Word?

15. Edwards says, "There is a language in actions. And in some cases the language of action is much more clear and convincing than words." Do you agree with this? Why or why not?

16. Is it possible to communicate the Gospel fully by actions and example? Why or why not?

VI. Subjects of It Are Guilty of Rash Acts and Unconventional Conduct

17. "The end for which God pours out His Spirit is to make men holy, and not to make them politicians." How does Edwards support this statement? Do you agree with him? Why or why not?

18. "If we see great rash acts and even sinful irregularities in some who are great instruments for carrying on the work, it will

not prove it *not* to be the work of God." Explain how Edwards supports this statement. How can you avoid becoming a hindrance to the work of the Spirit?

VII. ERRORS IN JUDGMENT AND DELUSIONS OF SATAN INTERMIX WITH THE WORK

19. What is the difference between the Spirit's work in the apostles and His work in revival?

VIII. SOME FALL AWAY INTO GROSS ERRORS OR SCANDALOUS PRACTICES

20. "If it appears that God has done a special work in someone and then that person falls away into gross errors or scandalous practices, that is no argument that the work in general is not the work of the Spirit of God." What reasons does Edwards give for saying this?

21. In what way is Jesus' relationship with Judas an example for guides in the visible church?

IX. MINISTERS PROMOTE IT BY THE TERRORS OF GOD'S HOLY LAW

22. Edwards asks, "Do we who have the care of souls know what hell is? Have we seen the state of the damned? Are we aware how dreadful their case is?" Write *your* answers to these questions in your journal.

23. "When ministers preach of hell and warn sinners to avoid it in a cold manner—though they may say in words that it is infinitely terrible—they contradict themselves." Do you agree? Why or why not?

24. "Some say it is unreasonable to frighten people into

heaven. But I think it is reasonable to try to frighten people away from hell." Do you agree? Why or why not?

> "Very often some text of Scripture expressing God's sovereignty has been impressed upon their minds. By this they have been calmed. They have been brought, as it were, to lie at God's feet. And after great agonies they have been composed and quiet in submission to a just and sovereign God" (Jonathan Edwards).

Write the following Scripture verse on a card and carry it with you. Read it aloud to yourself many times daily. Use it in your prayers.

> "The secret things belong to the LORD our God, but the things revealed belong to us and to our children forever, that we may follow all the words of this law" (Deuteronomy 29:29).

Write your response to the material for this session in light of the four filter questions on page 179.

Write your evaluation of this session after the discussion on the form provided by your leader.

As a result of praying, reading, writing, meeting, discussing, and doing what God encourages me to do from "Biblical Signs," I will be able to:

1. Define what a biblical sign is.

2. List the five biblical signs according to Edwards.

3. Explain these five biblical signs to another Christian.

Pray this prayer aloud each time you study.

Lord, revive my soul and revive the souls of my Key Covenant Teammates. Revive my church and my pastor. Lord, give me helpful insights and understanding from what I am about to study. Show me what I need to understand better. As You show me things I am eager to try, enable me to do them. As You show me things that I find hard to apply to my life, help me be honest about them. Lord, as I review the questions in the Discussion Guide, focus my mind and help me find the truth in what I study.

Write in your journal Edwards's five biblical signs.

Review the Table of Contents to see how "Biblical Signs" fits in with the whole work.

Read the following:

• Scan the four filter questions (page 179) to put your mind in a search mode.

• Read *The Spirit of Revival*, "Biblical Signs," pages 87-107.

• At least once, read aloud the Key Covenant, pages 170-173.

Section II: Biblical Signs: Distinguishing Scriptural Evidences of a Work of the Spirit of God

Write the answers to the following questions in your journal.

I. THE OPERATION EXALTS JESUS

1. What does the word *acknowledge* as it is often used in the New Testament mean?

2. The Holy Spirit inclines people's hearts to the historic Christ. What does Edwards say this means?

II. THE SPIRIT ATTACKS SATAN'S INTERESTS

3. What are the characteristics of Satan's kingdom?

4. What does the apostle John mean by "the world"?

5. Why does it not make sense to say that the devil may awaken men's consciences in order to deceive them?

6. Who is the person least likely to be deceived by the devil? Why?

III. THE SPIRIT EXALTS THE HOLY SCRIPTURES

7. How does Edwards explain the Spirit causing greater regard for the Holy Scriptures? Do you agree? Why or why not?

IV. THE SPIRIT LIFTS UP SOUND DOCTRINE

8. The true Spirit will convince people of what things?

9. When I see truth and am made aware of things as they really are, what is my duty?

V. The Spirit Promotes Love to God and Man

10. Edwards says, "Love is spoken of as if it were that of which the very nature of the Holy Spirit consists. It is as though divine love dwelling in us and the Spirit of God dwelling in us were the same thing." Do you agree? Why or why not?

11. "There is a counterfeit love that often appears among those who are led by a spirit of delusion." How does Edwards explain this? Do you agree? Why or why not?

12. From what does truly Christian love arise?

13. What is the surest character of true, divine, supernatural love, distinguishing it from the counterfeit?

14. What are the characteristics of "a person who dwells in love, who dwells in God and God in him"?

15. What does Christ's example teach us about the nature of God's love?

16. "Love and humility are the two things more contrary to the devil than anything in the world. The character of the devil, above all things, consists of pride and malice." Do you agree? Why or why not?

17. How does Edwards explain Satan masquerading as an angel of light? Do you agree? Why or why not?

"Very often some text of Scripture expressing God's sovereignty has been impressed upon their minds. By this they have been calmed. They have been brought, as it were, to lie at God's feet. And after great agonies they have been composed and quiet in submission to a just and sovereign God" (Jonathan Edwards).

Write the following Scripture verse on a card and carry it with you. Read it aloud to yourself many times daily. Use it in your prayers.

"I am the LORD, the God of all mankind. Is anything too hard for me?" (Jeremiah 32:27).

Write your response to the material for this session in light of the four filter questions on page 179.

Write your evaluation of this session after the discussion on the form provided by your leader.

SESSION FIVE

As a result of praying, reading, writing, meeting, discussing, and doing what God encourages me to do from "Practical Inferences," I will be able to:

1. List Edwards's three practical inferences.

2. Explain these three practical inferences to another Christian.

Pray this prayer aloud each time you study.

Lord, revive my soul and revive the souls of my Key Covenant Teammates. Revive my church and my pastor. Lord, give me helpful insights and understanding from what I am about to study. Show me what I need to understand better. As You show me things I am eager to try, enable me to do them. As You show me things that I find hard to apply to my life, help me be honest about them. Lord, as I review the questions in the Discussion Guide, focus my mind and help me find the truth in what I study.

Write in your journal Edwards's three practical inferences.

Review the Table of Contents to see how the "Practical Inferences" fit in with the whole.

Read the following:

• Scan the four filter questions (page 179) to put your mind in a search mode.

• Read *The Spirit of Revival*, "Practical Inferences," pages 109-150.

• At least once, read aloud the Key Covenant, pages 170-173.

Section III: Practical Inferences

Write the answers to the following questions in your journal.

I. THE RECENT EXTRAORDINARY INFLUENCE IS FROM THE SPIRIT OF GOD

1. What two things are needed to judge a work? What are two ways to compare facts with the rules?

2. Edwards says there were many things concerning the work in his day that were well-known and sufficient to determine it to be the work of God. What were these?

3. "But certainly there ought to be a distinction made between intense but fully proportional distress caused by fear of a terrifying truth and the effects produced by a needless and causeless fright." Do you agree? Why or why not?

4. "He is the God of order, not of confusion." How does Edwards explain this truth as it relates to the work of the "religious means"?

5. In the work of Edwards's day, what happened to the "formerly converted"? How open are you to something like this today in your life?

6. How does Edwards explain the presence of "rash acts, irregularities, and mixture of delusion"?

II. WE SHOULD DO OUR UTMOST TO PROMOTE IT

7. What reasons did Edwards give to urge Christians to support the work in his day?

8. "Silent ministers stand in the way of the work of God."

What did Edwards mean by this statement? Do you see examples of this today? Explain.

9. "They [who] wait to see a work of God without difficulties and stumbling blocks will be like a fool waiting at the riverside to have the water all run by. A work of God without stumbling blocks is never to be expected." Do you agree? Why?

10. What does Edwards say about the "excessively cautious ones [who] stand at a distance, doubting, wondering"? Do you agree? Why or why not?

11. "Those who do not become happier by it [the favor of God] will become far more guilty and miserable." Do you agree? Why or why not?

III. FRIENDS OF THIS WORK MUST GIVE DILIGENT HEED TO THEMSELVES

12. In what ways did Edwards urge friends of the work in his day to "give diligent heed to themselves"?

13. Why did Edwards expect that the great enemy of this work would try his utmost, especially with the friends of the work?

14. What is our best defense, and what does this imply we should do?

15. How does Edwards describe pride? Do you agree? Why or why not?

16. What counsel did Edwards give to those who were "giving too much heed to impulses and strong impressions on their minds"?

17. "A man may have those extraordinary gifts, yet be abominable to God and go to hell. The spiritual and eternal life of the

soul consists in the grace of the Spirit that God bestows only on His favorite and dear children. He has sometimes thrown out the other, as it were, to dogs and swine, as He did to Balaam, Saul, and Judas[2] and some who in the first times of the Christian church committed the unpardonable sin." Do you agree? Why or why not?

18. "The extraordinary gifts are worthless without the ordinary sanctifying influences." Do you agree? Why or why not?

19. "The apostle speaks of these gifts of inspiration as childish things in comparison to the influence of the Spirit in divine love. They are given to the church only to support it in its infancy. When the church should have a complete standing rule established and all the ordinary means of grace are settled, these gifts should cease as the church advances to the state of manhood." Do you agree? Why or why not?

20. "For my part, I had rather enjoy the sweet influences of the Spirit, I had rather show Christ's spiritual divine beauty, infinite grace, and dying love. I had rather draw forth the holy exercises of faith, divine love, sweet complacence, and humble joy in God. I had rather experience all this for one quarter of an hour than to have prophetical visions and revelations the whole year." Do you agree? Why or why not?

21. "I know by experience that impressions made with great power upon the minds of true and eminent saints are no sure signs of their being revelations from heaven. . . . They who leave that word to follow such impressions and impulses leave the guidance of the polar star to follow a man with a lamp." Do you agree? Why or why not?

22. "Study is the means of obtaining knowledge. So if we are not to despise knowledge obtained by human means, then it will

follow that we are not to neglect study. Furthermore, study is of great use to prepare for publicly instructing others." Do you agree? Why or why not?

23. How far do the rules of the Holy Scriptures truly justify our passing censures upon other professing Christians?

24. "The longer I live, the less I wonder that God keeps it as His right to try the hearts of the children of men. Also I wonder less that God directs that this business should be let alone till harvest. I adore the wisdom of God! In His goodness to me and my fellow creatures, He has not committed this great business into our hands. We are such poor, weak, and dim-sighted creatures. We are so blind, full of pride, partial, prejudiced, and deceitful of heart. So He has committed it into the hands of One infinitely fitter for it and has made it His own right." Do you agree? Why or why not?

25. "God has established a regular ecclesiastical proceeding for discipline in His visible church," teaching that no one has a right to exclude anyone from this visible church except in this way. Do you agree? Why or why not?

26. "It is proper for Christians to be like lambs who are not apt to complain and cry when they are hurt. It becomes Christians to be dumb and not to open their mouths after the example of our dear Redeemer." Do you agree? Why or why not?

27. "I believe we have confined ourselves too much to a certain stated method and form in the management of our religious affairs. This has tended to cause all our Christian faith to degenerate into mere formality." Is this a danger today? Explain.

28. "Whatever has the appearance of a great innovation tends greatly to hinder the progress of the power of the Christian faith.

These innovations tend to greatly shock and surprise people's minds. They set people talking and disputing. They raise the opposition of some and divert the minds of others. These innovations perplex many with doubts and scruples. They cause people to swerve from their great business and turn aside to vain jangling. Therefore, these great innovations, unless they are of considerable importance, are best avoided." Is this a danger today? Explain.

> **"Very often some text of Scripture expressing God's sovereignty has been impressed upon their minds. By this they have been calmed. They have been brought, as it were, to lie at God's feet. And after great agonies they have been composed and quiet in submission to a just and sovereign God" (Jonathan Edwards).**

Write the following Scripture verse on a card and carry it with you. Read it aloud to yourself many times daily. Use it in your prayers.

> **"Ah, Sovereign LORD, you have made the heavens and the earth by your great power and outstretched arm. Nothing is too hard for you" (Jeremiah 32:17).**

Write your response to the material for this session in light of the four filter questions on page 179.

Write your evaluation of this session after the discussion on the form provided by your leader.

SESSION SIX

As a result of praying, reading, writing, meeting, discussing, and doing what God encourages me to do from reviewing and evaluating *The Spirit of Revival* I will be able to:

1. Provide helpful insights to improve future Key Covenant Teams.

2. Determine what my participation in an ongoing Key Covenant Fellowship will be.

Pray this prayer aloud each time you study.

Lord, revive my soul and revive the souls of my Key Covenant Teammates. Revive my church and my pastor. Lord, give me helpful insights and understanding from what I am about to study. Show me what I need to understand better. As You show me things I am eager to try, enable me to do them. As You show me things that I find hard to apply to my life, help me be honest about them. Lord, as I review the questions in the Discussion Guide, focus my mind and help me find the truth in what I study.

Read the following:

• Scan the four filter questions (page 179) to put your mind in a search mode.

• Read *The Spirit of Revival*, Epilogue, pages 153-158.

Write the answers to the following questions in your journal.

1. Watching for revival requires staying awake, staying alert, and staying alive. What should this mean in your life and ministry for the Lord?

2. What are the three things suggested for monthly Key Covenant Fellowship meetings?

3. What is the process for developing an ongoing fellowship of people (KCF) who are praying for revival, seeking personal renewal, and working for church revitalization?

4. What part do you believe God would have you take in this ongoing process of the Key Covenant Fellowship in your church?

Review now *The Spirit of Revival.*

"Very often some text of Scripture expressing God's sovereignty has been impressed upon their minds. By this they have been calmed. They have been brought, as it were, to lie at God's feet. And after great agonies they have been composed and quiet in submission to a just and sovereign God" (Jonathan Edwards).

Write the following Scripture verse on a card and carry it with you. Read it aloud to yourself many times daily. Use it in your prayers.

"In him we were also chosen, having been predestined according to the plan of him who works out everything in conformity with the purpose of his will" (Ephesians 1:11).

Write your response to the material for this session in light of the four filter questions on page 179.

Write your evaluation of this session after the discussion and your evaluation of this Key Covenant Team experience on the form provided by your leader.

FOOTNOTES TO THIS SECTION

1. "When he takes the throne of his kingdom, he is to write for himself on a scroll a copy of this law, taken from that of the priests, who are Levites. It is to be with him, and he is to read it all the days of his life so that he may learn to revere the LORD his God and follow carefully all the words of this law and these decrees" (Deuteronomy 17:18-19).

2. Balaam—see Numbers 22—24; Saul—see 1 Samuel 10:10-11; Judas, numbered with the Twelve—see Matthew 10:2-5. "These twelve Jesus sent out with the following instructions: 'Do not go among the Gentiles or enter any town of the Samaritans. Go rather to the lost sheep of Israel. As you go, preach this message: "The kingdom of heaven is near." Heal the sick, raise the dead, cleanse those who have leprosy, drive out demons. Freely you have received, freely give.'"

A Leader's Guide is available to you to facilitate your Key Covenant Team meetings. You may order this guide by writing, calling, faxing, or e-mailing:

Archie Parrish

Serve International

4646 North Shallowford Road

Suite 200

Atlanta, GA 30338

770-642-2449

FAX 770-642-4195

Parrish7@aol.com

SCRIPTURE INDEX

GENERAL INDEX